In Praise of Ruin's Wheel

"This intriguing book, part memoir by a father and son separated by 60 years of history, part academic treatise on war, genocide, and the Holocaust, is a must for anyone looking to find an introduction to these issues at at time when, more than ever, they are in our daily consciousness."

Jon Blair
Writer, producer and director of the Academy Award and Emmy winning documentary *Anne Frank Remembered*; the British Academy Award winning *Schindler: The True Story*; and the Emmy winning series *Reporters at War*.

"There is hardly any essay that so successfully explores the permanent problems facing mankind in so few pages."

Gottfried H. Wagner
Musicologist and human rights activist and author of *Twilight of the Wagners: The Unveiling of a Family Legacy*.

"Neither conventional history nor standard survivor's memoir, *Ruin's Wheel* is a Dutchman's chronicle and reflection on the shocking epoch in Dutch history and its aftermath—when the Germans marched into Holland in the early morning of May 10, 1940, and his son's desire to set his text in the context of genocide. Part One is a moving "thrice born" account of Jan Colijn, Dean of General Studies, the Richard Stockton College of New Jersey: his natal origins in descriptions of boyhood and adolescent years in Holland; his life in America to pursue graduate work and ultimately an academic career; and, at the death of his mother, his return home to encounter again the painful cycle of WW II memories. Part Two is Izaak Colijn's testimonial diary, which speaks to the function and dysfunction of the Dutch state and society during the Nazi years. Part Three and the book's Appendix elaborate on Jewish victimization and genocidal acts then and now, and attempt a detailed answer to "What Have We Learned about Genocide?" What emerges from *pater et fils* is that ever-n-again "thinking people" are the surest antidote to societal evil. *Ruin's Wheel* is a reader-friendly, invaluable first-person psycho-sociological discussion of why the Shoah (Holocaust) and genocide matters."

Zev Garber
Professor and Chair of Jewish Studies, Los Angeles Valley College and co-author of *Double Takes: Thinking and Rethinking Issues of Modern Judaism in Ancient Contexts* (University Press of America, 2004) and editor and contributor, *Mel Gibson's Passion: the Film, the Controversy, and Its Implications* (Purdue University Press, 2006).

RUIN'S WHEEL

A father on war, a son on genocide

G. Jan Colijn and Izaak Colijn

COMTEQ
PUBLISHING
MARGATE, NEW JERSEY

Published by:
 ComteQ Publishing
 A division of ComteQ Communications, LLC
 P.O. Box 3046
 Margate, New Jersey 08402
 609-487-9000 • Fax 609-822-4098
 Email: publisher@ComteQcom.com
 Website: www.ComteQpublishing.com

ISBN10 0-9766889-5-6
ISBN13 978-0-9766889-5-2
Library of Congress Control Number: 2006920567

Book design by Rob Huberman
Cover design by Gary D. Schenck
The extract from Reveille is included with the kind permission of The Society of Authors as the Literary Representative of the Estate of A.E. Housman.

Printed in the United States of America
10 9 8 7 6 5 4 3 2 1

In memory of
Arie Duiker and Max Koopman

CONTENTS

PREFACE

Jung Chang and Jon Halliday recently published the book *Mao: the Unknown Story*. It reminds us that stories about the Holocaust, and about genocide in general, were written by many more people—the perpetrators who caused them. These stories are then read by many others, but they are a perpetual nightmare for those having to remember them.

Conversely, some – once fanatically active and involved—prefer to ignore their activism and involvement later on. In Germany, "Wir haben es nicht gewüßt" (we really did not know) metamorphoses into "Good night, don't let the bed bugs bite." When those "bed bugs" are one's own consciouness, this is cowardly denial, an effort to sleep calmly and, as it was once written, "go gently into that good night." However, the tears of the past are still the reality of today, just as long as men continue to eat apples from their neighbors' trees and conceal doing so. Thanks to people like Geert Jan Colijn, there is no escape from the stories of the Holocaust and genocide. The bugs are still there!

Thus, books like this contribute to build the foundation of a just society in the future. Thanks to Geert Jan Colijn, neither the memories nor the bugs will fade or fly away, and that will allow all of us to learn, and do better, always better in the future—for a just society for our children.

Jack H. Koopman
Amsterdam
January, 2006

Introduction

My mother, Aaltje Colijn-Rozeboom, passed away in 1998, well into her nineties. For more than a half century she had lived in the five bedroom house in The Netherlands where I grew up, and she was a thrifty pack rat. Thank goodness for that because, emptying the house, I found the unpublished World War II memoirs of my father, Izaak Colijn. That was a surprise because it is his only unpublished manuscript. My father taught English for a living, but wrote for a life. In the last few years of his life, for example, he published *Rambles in Britain* (1953), *England and the English* (1954), *With the M.M.S. to England* (1956), *Engels voor de H.B.S – A* (1957), *Walks and Talks in the Fields of English literature* (1958), and *An Introduction to Shakespeare* (1958). Most of his works aimed to teach translation to students in various high school tracks and to introduce England, its people, its literature, its cities and countryside—all equally loved—to Dutch teenagers in such a way that they, too, would enjoy it. He penned everything in long hand. A partner in his publisher's firm, *W.J. Thieme en Cie*, would pick up the manuscripts and take them to Zutphen, where the company was housed.

Many of the books had multiple editions but they did not make him rich. There is a saying of German origin that publishers drink champagne from the skulls of scholars. Well, Dad did not drink (or smoke) so he can't have been too upset, but his royalties were certainly modest in light of the many editions of the widely used books, a gravy train for *Thieme*. They continued to publish his work after my father died, with a new editor. So it goes.

Why this recently discovered manuscript was unpublished is a bit of a mystery, given my father's role as rain maker for *Thieme*. It is likely that the early post-war years were not the best time to publish war memoirs. The country was busy with reconstruction, the general mood was to draw a line under World War II, and there was silence about central aspects of the war, especially the fate of Dutch Jews. War memory consisted of a simple dichotomy: harsh German occupation and heroic Dutch resistance; much more about that soon.

There was more to my father than teaching and writing. He was a Renaissance man. I am sure I knew that as a kid, but I shrugged such things off, then. It did not intimidate me. It did not weigh on me. Only when time became more precious in middle age did I fully understand his range and productivity, and only after my parents' house was emptied after my mother's death did it hit me all at once.

There was his Stradivarius, more than a hundred years old now but factory made (it won't make us rich). There were his drawings and etchings that startle house guests because they evoke Rembrandt. There were his track and field medals. He did not medal in the Olympics but he was a good "third man" on the Dutch 4x100 squad. He took me to meet long distance track legend Emil Zatopek when I was around six years old, an unforgettable experience.[1]

There was a box of records, all 78 rpm, all mono, recorded by him during a brief span in the early 1950s. A few years ago they were turned into a double CD set, and now I can bear to listen to them again. The records contain a good deal of Schubert. The *Lieder* suited his baritone range, but also his self-effacing quietude. There are Bach arias where a listener can, I think, hear his particular and deep religiosity, ill-fitted to the dourness of the Dutch Reformed Church. He "belonged," though he would mostly just "go" to conduct choirs. His relation with God was very much one-on-one. There is a nice energy when my father is accompanied by his son Piet, my brother, a teenager at the time, a budding shot putter and discus thrower, though you would not know it from his soft touch on the piano.

My father, when he was not writing, drawing, or grading, would listen to music, shuffle his score sheets, and he would practice his scales every morning in front of an open window in his study. He loved the choir work and he organized the production of recordings of his pupils singing or acting in a Shakespeare play. Now which English teacher would say to his pupils: "Here is the Merchant of Venice, Act V, scene 1. You are Jessica. Take it from 'In such a night. Did Thisbe fearfully o'er-trip the dew...' and, by the way, we are recording"? Recording?! Immortality and Fame! We lived in the Dutch Hollywood, surrounded by radio and television stations: records were the currency of cool, and on the records you can hear the excited intent with which the young voices go about their paces. There is some fine teaching going on.

My father lost his fight with cancer in 1959—a fight he did not know he was in. It was a stupendous waste and it left me quite angry for many years. Listening to his voice today is a sweet comfort but it does not grasp the entire man. There simply were too many sides to him. In the Bible he got from his mother upon confirmation she wrote: "*Izaak—wees altijd braaf.*" *Braaf* is a broad anachronism for good, obedient, decent. Dad was all that. He had great faith in God but mostly went to church just to conduct. He did not like his faith mediated by the formalities of church organization.

Former students would stay in touch with him all his life. He was handsome. He was an artist. He was strict but kind. He was beloved.

When I came across his war memoirs, I realized I would have to "do something" with them, in due time. I was born after the war but, for a host of reasons, I have had a personal and professional life centered a good deal on World War II. So the idea for this book eventually emerged as two stories on the war, his based on experience, mine on post-war reflections. You will find him the better writer so, if you get through Part I, The Weight, you will know I owe him for that writing gene, too, and you will know the best part is yet to come.

I wrote this book with an eye on the so-called "third generation," the grandchildren of those who experienced the war, now finishing high school, in college, or a bit older. This is a generation that has a different, less emotional take on World War II than the "second" generation, my contemporaries, who grew up in the shadow of the war.

My generation, especially the children of victims or perpetrators of atrocities, often has a complex and emotionally difficult relationship with the war, if not with our parents, especially parents guilty of wrong-doing. Thus, I also wrote for my oldest and closest mate, in Yiddish my *gabber:* his name is Jack, a Dutch Jew, a child of survivors. But this story grew because of later friends as well: Yair, a Polish born Jew, and Gottfried, the great-grandson of Richard Wagner. We have all spent years digesting the war—and still do so. Others became part of the narrative for a variety of reasons. They sometimes appear remarkably unaffected by the war, probably a blessing to them but also to me. They help me gain perspective.

I hope the stories will be a small contribution to an understanding of what happened in the war from a Dutch perspective, and to understanding how some of the middle generation learned to cope with the years that would define us in various degrees. As that journey unfolded we found a few shards of wisdom worth sharing with the next generation: a few thoughts on how we may deal not only with the Holocaust and the broader canvas of genocide, but also some reflections on nettlesome perennials—racism, nationalism, violence, and warfare, in their current manifestations.

One thread in this book not explicitly addressed warrants a brief note here. Grappling with history is like pushing beads of mercury. What appeared as self-evident truth in 1945 is now written off as nonsense. The narrative constantly evolves; history is constantly reconstructed. Therefore, today's students are well advised to accept any prevailing current truths about our own world with more than a grain of salt: a generation from now, today's truisms may well look tragically wrong in retrospect. In the same vein, those not actually present in the past must guard against sitting in rear-view mirrored judgment on those present at the time. Hindsight choices are always easier to make than current ones.

A few words on my father's memoirs, a long essay, really. I found it difficult to decide whether to edit it for publication. After all, he would have done so, I am sure, because he was a careful and conscientious craftsman. But I decided to leave the text as is. It was a decision from the heart, not from the head. I simply felt that I had no right to superimpose my style on his by editing his work. Leaving the text alone means that you will read the odd inconsistency: 8 or ten days, not eight or ten days; % here, percentage there. I think the text speaks more true as it is, more immediate and direct, as it were, and that is the way it should be. I know full well it would have been error proof if he had seen it to publication himself but I like the rawness of the draft.

Though he writes that these memoirs were not meant to be a book, his essay addresses an English audience. He wrote in English, not American English, so it is *neighbour* not *neighbor*, *burgomaster*, not *mayor, to-day* (at that time) not always *today, aeroplanes,* often abbreviated as *'planes.*

What struck me most, however, were not these details but learning about the sheer terror and brutality of occupation in new ways. I, for one, had no idea that teachers were sent to concentration camps when their charges beat up class mates whose parents were Nazis. It must have been utterly terrifying to go to work, knowing your life may depend on what boys and girls in your class may do—and those were the good ones, mind you.

You will read of his exasperation about the foolishness of the Dutch government-in-exile when it ordered a railway strike late in the war to thwart the German war effort, a strike that had had no effect on the Germans but was exploited by them, a strike also that had as its unintended consequence a very severe food shortage.[2]

You can certainly feel the emasculation of complying time and again with Nazi regulations, for example, promising not to engage in sabotage or declaring one is not a Jew, but the most frightening must have been the fear of sudden round-ups (*razzias*) of able-bodied men for the purpose of deportation into forced labor.

You may think differently about your next meal after reading about the obsessive struggle to find food when shortages reached such levels that people ate tulip bulbs.

But you also will enjoy the poetic exhilaration when liberation came at last, and my father's deep gratitude to the Almighty.

The folder wherein my Dad kept his manuscript and other war documentation has a nice cover he designed for it, with the title *of War and Peace 1940-45*. But the manuscript itself had a different title, with a line from Robert Burns's poem *"Strathallan's Lament,"* "Ruin's wheel has driven o'er us" slightly altered to *When ruin's wheel rolled o'er us.* How very apt.

I am indebted to friends and colleagues at The Richard Stockton College of New Jersey, historians Michael Hayse and Paul Lyons, political science colleagues Alan Arcuri, Bill Daly, Patrick Hossay, and Bill Sensiba, economists Erkan Alpan, Reza Ghorashi, Melaku Lakew, and sociologist David Emmons. All provide interesting windows on the world. Of particular value have been visiting Holocaust scholars, such as Hubert Locke, Yehuda Bauer, and Dan Bar-On. I have been stimulated by our own Holocaust scholar, Sister Carol Rittner, R.S.M., the "flying nun," by film maker Jon Blair, who became a close personal friend though he supports Arsenal (I belong to a different church), and by Dutch historians Nanda van der Zee and Dienke Hondius. They all have helped shape my thinking on several subjects in this book. I am grateful to the College's head librarian, David Pinto, who helped trace the provenance of books I had originally read in Dutch translation a long time ago. Thanks also to Ken Tompkins and Tom Kinsella who traced down the Robert Burns' poem from which my father derived his title.

I want to thank especially a former colleague, Mimi Schwartz, Professor of Writing *emerita* at my institution who read the earliest version of this draft and brought me the insight of a professional writer together with her wisdom as a member of the "second generation." I am indebted to my staff, Peggy Rivera, Claire Lopatto, Vicki Cantell, and students Jennifer Garsh and Sarah Collura, who protected their dean for an hour or so each day so that I could work on this book without interruptions. I have benefited a lot from the work of the staff in our Holocaust Resource Center, Gail Rosenthal and Maryann McLoughlin. Maryann also proofread a draft and compiled the endnotes.

Long-standing personal friends, first Jack Koopman and then Roselien Vecht, are at the genesis of the story. Pieter Lakeman, Willem Langenberg, Paul Verberne, and especially Peter Heyen helped hone my thinking at university. They taught me a few other things, too, best left out of this book. Friends acquired later, especially Gottfried Wagner and Yair Cohen, have been wonderful sounding boards for the past few decades.

Most of all, I am grateful to my parents who gave me a pretty good idea about what is important to value in life, concern with the world beyond one's direct environment, loyalty, frankness, a good work ethic, and a taste for humor, among others. Not much in my life would have meaning without my wife, Sarah, and our daughter, Cory, who are not just a seamless continuance to friends and parents but an apotheosis of everything that is good around me. I am a pretty privileged fellow.

Of course, this book's flaws are entirely mine: rest assured that all those just acknowledged are not responsible. Rest assured they may well have tried but many Dutchmen are a bit headstrong: I probably did not listen well enough to what they had to say.

G. Jan Colijn, Port Republic 2006

PART ONE

The Weight

The Weight

Naarden

"With *that* boy you will not play." My mother's right hand was pointing like a handgun, index finger angrily extended as a boy cycled by our house. His name was Gert Jan and he was a year ahead of me. I was eight and older namesakes—well, I had an extra *e* in Geert—are of interest at that age. What was this all about? Was this one of those dirty boys you begin to hear about before you are a teen, even in the prudish 1950s? The answer did not wait long. The boy's father, my mother explained, had been a Dutch SS volunteer. She insisted he had fought in Finland, and she remembered with graphic precision how he tried to sink his SS uniform in the pond in front of our old house, across the *Rijksweg*, the main national road, which split the neighborhood. The sinking took place on *Dolle Dinsdag*, Mad Tuesday, when the news of the D-day landing (June 6, 1944) had reached Nazi occupied Holland, an exciting day for the Dutch though not quite as jolly for Nazi sympathizers. Our SS man had made a mess of things. The uniform simply refused to go down, to the jeers of the neighborhood. I shrugged off the news. My social loss was tempered. The boy was not very good at soccer; otherwise, there may have been an argument.

I was getting used to my mother's admonitions: her landscape was divided between those she rated "good" in the war and rated "*fout*," literally meaning wrong, the new term for anybody who had collaborated with the Nazis or profited from the war. She seemed to know them all. There was her Uncle Willem, the only black sheep Nazi sympathizer among eight brothers and sisters, an object of scorn but also pride because he was the exception. Also, he had done nothing really wrong, just been wrong-headed. He would die young and that ended the issue. The aunt was rehabilitated over time, more or less. There was a green-grocer who had supplied the troops; the family who had sold electrical equipment to the Nazis; and the butcher who in the Hunger Winter of 1944 (see note 2) said he would only have meat for my mother in exchange for sex. My mother always bristled telling that one. She had turned him down but her sense of violation was tangible a decade later.

The good/wrong fault line seeped into virtually all aspects of daily life. I grew up in a musical family. My father, Izaak, played violin, my mother, Aaltje, and brother, Piet, piano; I was learning the flute, but more central was that my father, who made a living teaching English and writing books, made a life by conducting choirs and by recording. He was a fine, lyrical baritone with a penchant for Bach, Schubert and Mendelssohn. Many mornings he would practice, running scales in front of an open window in his study. An example of that fault line was the stewardship of the Concertgebouw Orchestra. Recordings under Willem Mengelberg, the authoritarian music director, a forceful giant in the Karajan or Toscanini mold, were not bought. If they played on the radio we were reminded that he had conducted during the war, as the orchestra was stripped of its Jewish musicians, and had toured as well. He was, therefore, no good, and the orchestra's performances were too dramatic as well. In contrast, his successor, Eduard van Beinum, was revered as a smart but pleasant and modest man whose public persona and appearance resembled my father's. He had worked during the war but very reluctantly and as little as possible and was openly opposed to the Nazis. Not surprisingly he was considered "good." After his sudden death in April 1959—within days of the equally untimely death of my father—we transferred our loyalties to Bernard Haitink with ease. Like van Beinum he was free of megalomania. He also lived nearby and you support the home side. Based on our views of Germanic style, and presumed or known wartime behavior, Elisabeth Schwarzkopf was not played at home, but the subdued beauty of Dietrich Fischer-Dieskau's singing passed muster. Wagner—and more about him later—was too bombastic and Wagner's influence on Hitler was fully understood.

The war not only contoured our judgment based upon what we thought others did or did not do in the war, it shaped our behavior. We did not vacation in Germany though my parents had gone there on honeymoon in the 1930s. Ian Buruma speculates that the Dutch upper-middle class was simply Anglophile, unlike the lower class, and, given my father's occupation, Anglophile we certainly were. We did not buy German goods and the breakthrough on that score did not come until the 1970s when I bought my mother her first Braun coffee maker. My Uncle Kees did drive a VW and would do so most of his life. We were not sure about that one. He also had some German friends in *Naturfreunde* (friends of nature) circles. We treated them with polite indifference. We had no German friends. All our foreign friends were English and there was a steady stream of visitors, from teachers to test drivers.

In summers, it was a boy's job to give wrong directions to Germans vacationing in Holland, bound for the beaches where they may, no *must* have served in the bunkers of the Atlantic Wall during the war. We had an uncanny sense of where the east was and to the east we pointed. We cursed those who put *Zimmer frei* (room available) signs on their rentals: post-war profiteers!

We were unreservedly pro-Israel, certainly up to the 1967 war.[3] We loved Israel-the-underdog and the image of Israel was of a nation with nothing but progressive Zionists. To us, a *kibbutz* was a kind of socialist summer camp. These images only began to show nuance when Israel became an occupying state. Occupation we knew, and after 1967 and then 1973 Dutch views on Israel became not just more nuanced but positively muddled. The length of the Palestianian-Israeli conflict seems to lead to compassion fatigue and exasperation, leading to indifference, inimical to "a plague on both your houses." As elsewhere, there emerges over time less and less breathing space for those who remain genuinely concerned with the fate of Jews, yet critical of certain policies of successive Israeli governments. There is simply no wiggle room because of the competition of two narratives, one pro-Israel, one pro-Palestine. The group in the middle, those conflicted, is chastised as philosemitic for their concerns with Jews in one narrative, and as antisemitic in the other narrative.

My parents' politics were left of center. My mother remembered the abject poverty in Drenthe, the province of her youth where peat farmers had lived in huts. It had made an indelible impression on her. Politics in our house were mildly pacifist, socialist and anti-communist, anti-fascist, anti-clerical (the Catholic Church, we were told, did nothing about the poor while enriching itself with their contributions), and anti-authoritarian because fascism and communism favored the strong man. For that reason, Hendrik Colijn, repeatedly prime minister before the war, was despised not only for his strict Christian politics, but also because he was a strong man. It did not help that he had fired women civil servants during the Depression, including mother who was a teacher, as a way to ameliorate male unemployment. A woman's place was in the home, a man's place on the job. A relative he may have been but mother never forgave him.

A few more words on Colijn are in order. He was prime minister in four successive Dutch governments between 1933 and 1939, a leader faced with enormous problems: the challenge of growing Dutch National Socialist extremism, the stirrings of independence in the Dutch East Indies, an international situation worsening each year by an ever more aggressive Hitler Germany (and fascist Italy), and the economic crisis of the 1930s with its massive unemployment. Governing from the right, he outmaneuvered the ultra-right, the Dutch Nazis. His economic policies were not as successful. He was a fiscal conservative who did not like government deficit spending as a way out of the economic crisis as the economist John Maynard Keynes proposed, an idea that was implemented in several neighboring countries. He was a man who understood that strong leadership in crises finds electoral resonance even if the remedies don't work, and he was leading a country that, having escaped the instability of World War I when the country was neutral, was not quite ready for radical political or economic reform. He was authoritarian, with reservations about the parliamentary part of the Dutch system of parliamentary democracy but he also rejected Nazism.

After the occupation began (he had been out of office for a while already) he started to give lectures that hinted at moral resistance to the Nazi occupation. The Nazis found him dangerous, and subsequently he was exiled to Germany where he died in 1944.

I inherited the strong anti-authoritarian views of my mother, and so I was not very fond of Colijn in my youth but there was something else, too. When you share a last name with a prominent, dominant politician, people think you are of the same persuasion. That would make me an authoritarian, strict Calvinist conservative. I am not. The scarlet letter of that shared last name has been an irritant all my life: the prominence of the name often opens doors, but, for me, they are the wrong doors.

Finally, we were not very royalist although Queen Juliana's palace was just a stone's throw from my parents' house in Soest before the war. My father had occasion to meet Wilhelmina, the Queen's predecessor, and found her remote and disdainful toward commoners. Dutch royals had married Germans for several generations; it did not go unnoticed. Wilhelmina's husband was viewed as a philanderer and a drunk. Rumor had it that Wilhelmina used to scold him for drinking beer from a company other than the one wherein she held stock. The politics of Juliana's Bernhard were suspect. Sure, he was revered among some Dutch resistance veterans but to us German nobility could not possibly be pro-democratic and his heavy accent, a life-long affliction, only added to that stereotype. Moreover, he had the panache of a playboy, with a taste for fast cars and fast women, then a rumor, later affirmed: extra-marital offspring did not fit the values of my parents. My father was more deferential to authority than my mother who bristled at any authority, especially authority based on royal heredity, but anti-royalism did not extend to other nobility. After my parents' house was bombed in an air raid, they moved in with an Esquire, and many years later, there was a Baron and a Lady at my wedding. My hometown was near all Dutch radio and, later, television studios. Despite my parents' politics I grew up a bit of a snob.

The war shaped behavior and judgment but also ritual. We religiously attended the silent processional on May 4 each year, a commemoration of the fallen that started at a small monument a few yards from our house where some poor Dutchmen had been mowed down in a German reprisal action. On May 5, the flag came out to celebrate the liberation of 1945. One of our jokes was about a German tourist who had asked a Jewish survivor what this silent parade was all about. Moos (male Jews in Dutch jokes are either Moos or Sam) had said: "Today we remember all the victims of the second World War." The German responded: "We lost a lot of Germans in the war, too." "Yes," Moos said, "and that we celebrate tomorrow!"

World War II was the plumb line in the lives of my parents' generation, the event whereon the compass was drawn. Their generation had also lived through World War I but they had been little, and The Netherlands had been neutral during the war: WW I had passed us by and would not enter the nation's memory in the same way it did in Britain, France, or in the mind of a young veteran, Adolf Hitler. In

Holland WW I was history. However, WW II was over, but not done with. World War II was the tableau upon which family histories were drawn, the roof from under which we viewed the world. Historian Martin Conway notes a similarity in his "The Memory of the Second World War in Flanders." The war served "as point of reference for the private world of family memory."

Two threads ran through every family anecdote: war was a dance with Providence and my generation should be happy because we had not been around.

My family was not disproportionately victimized. On my mother's side there was the loss of much beloved cousin Arie, a victim of forced labor, the *Arbeitseinsatz*. When the call-ups of boys older than eighteen began in 1943, Arie signed up early, not out of any pro-German conviction but because he told his father: "I might as well go instead of a father with children." His father implored him to go into hiding but Arie fatalistically thought he should take his chances and just go. He was put to work in a poisonous chemicals plant near Bremen, came home for a leave once, was begged to go underground again, returned to Germany and died of typhoid fever. Sanitary provisions in the camp were dreadful including bad drinking water. The Nazis tried to bury him with a swastika flag on his casket but his fellow prisoners removed it.

Mother's Aunt Korrie and her husband, Aart, had a hell of a war, but not in Germany. Aart was an officer in the Dutch East Indies Army and they were both interned when Japan's occupation began. Those camps were not extermination camps but they came close. Mortality figures were extremely high. The English speaking world learned about such allied prisoner camps through such films as *The Bridge over the River Kwaï* and the situation in women's camps found its way into Helen Colijn's *Song of Survival*, which became the movie *Paradise Road*, with Glenn Close. I learned about the camps at home. Aunt Korrie told me about the punishment of prisoners, how they were strapped over a hole with fast-growing bamboo punctuating their backs until they would faint after days under the hot tropical sun.

For most others in the family the war had been a matter of narrow escapes. There was the radio turned to the BBC, silenced and hidden just in time when the knock on the door came. There was a narrow escape when the Germans pulled an ammunition train into Naarden, our home town, figuring that the allies would not bomb a Dutch residential area. Wrong. They did, and my parents' house was severely damaged. They got out alive. Among my prized possessions was a bomb shard given to me when I was little. Still have it, too.

Cousin Piet was picked up in an *Arbeitseinsatz razzia* (round-ups for forced labor) after school, and put on an eastbound train to Amersfoort. He calmly pried loose a board in the train wagon, lowered himself down to the railroad ties, let go, and walked home where he got a good cuffing from his mother for being late for dinner. Piet's father, Uncle Gerard, would lose his legs during a bombing raid near The Hague but he lived. Alas, he could not work in the restaurant business again, so he opened a tobacco shop after the war.

One day Cousin Frans Maas and his little boy, Connie, were walking on a dike near Westkapelle on the island of Walcheren. Walcheren was at the mouth of the Scheldt River, which led to the strategically important Belgian port Antwerp. The allies began a bombing campaign late in the war. Inundating Walcheren, which is below sea level, would impede the manoeuvres of German troops. Frans and Connie were caught in a sudden raid and started to run toward a windmill along the dike. Connie stumbled as the bombs started exploding. They never made it to the windmill. Good thing: the windmill took a direct hit and there were no survivors.

These anecdotes made clear that war was a matter of compressed fate. The war had been a fearful five years; the family had suffered yet mostly survived. The suffering was impressed upon us especially in terms of food shortages. Mother, when neither Dad nor my brother could go on the street, would ride a bicycle without tires (Germans had requisitioned all rubber) for miles in search of food, and in the Hunger Winter of 1944 they, too, ate tulip bulbs (see note 2). Of course, after the war we always had to finish our plates. No food was ever thrown out, a habit not overcome until I reached middle age in my adopted America where food issues run quite a different gamut.

Family stories were invariably handled with an affective stroke over my head and a lesson: "Be happy you weren't there." That one was more problematic. When we were very young we were rather upset we missed the show, though we did not dare say so out loud. Our heroes were icons of the resistance, or the commander of the Dutch fleet, Karel Doorman, who had led Dutch naval forces against the Japanese (and considerable odds) in the Java Sea, joining a rich tradition of Dutch maritime heroes going all the way back to the sixteenth century and the Dutch war for independence against Spain.

I imagined myself a British flying ace in the Battle for Britain or even, having read about a legless hero such as Douglas Bader in Paul Brickhill's book, *The Great Escape*, as a valiant POW in a *Stalag* (prisoner of war camp) making a nuisance of myself—a role my teachers would agree was a natural for me. I read about D-Day until there were no books left to read and everything I could get my hands on about the Battle of the Bulge.[4] Until I learned more about his antisemitism decades later, Patton was another hero.[5] I visited his statue in Luxemburg and saluted every time I drove by as a student in America when the cheapest transatlantic flights were Icelandic Air out of Luxemburg. I was ten when a summer camp took us near Maastricht and also Malmédy. There they were: endless, rolling hills of white crosses and an occasional star of David, row after row of sacrifice. Seeing that, and reading about Stalingrad, left little doubt about the carnage of war.[6] But in youthful dreams and fantasy, we did not die, we were heroes and lived. Did not Monty say on D-Day:

> *He either fears his fate too much*
> *Or his desires are small*
> *Who dare not put it to the touch*
> *To win or lose it all.*[7]

My God, we had missed our chance at glory and we deeply rued the day we were born, too late. Only when not day-dreaming and over time did we learn to understand that war is hell.

Ian Buruma contends that our contemporaries could envision ourselves heroes in the war because the post-war Dutch ignored the nation's shameful compliance and collaboration with the implementation of the Holocaust in the Netherlands. Until the 1960s that was certainly true: the destruction of Dutch Jewry, disproportionate as it was among occupied countries in western Europe, was ignored through denial or with the kind of incomprehension and indifference, bordering on hostility, that Dienke Hondius sketches in *The Return,* a book on the reception of repatriated camp survivors. Ido de Haan wrote on the same subject in a book titled *Na de ondergang: De Herinnering aan de Jodenvervolging in Nederland 1945-1955* (*After the Destruction: The Memory of the Persecution of Jews in the Netherlands 1945-1955*). Victims, unlike resistance fighters, were not heroes. They were told to get on with it. Moreover, the Dutch, it was said, suffered, too.

There is a good reason for such denial: if the Dutch memories of the war were a matter of "good" and "*fout*" and if the most comfortable Dutch self-image was seeing the war as one between terrible German occupation and Dutch resistance, then the fate of the Jews could not easily fit in the narrative. The realization that especially Dutch officials had been Hitler's willing neighbors would not come until the late 1960s, and thereafter. In my house, however, the Holocaust was not ignored and that had little to do with the fact that mother once had been a *sjabbes* goy—a gentile who helped Jews with chores they could not do on the Sabbath.

The Holocaust mattered because we had a close bruise with destiny related to it, and lived to tell the tale. Father had troubled intestines all his life. He would die of cancer in his duodenal tract, a cancer which spread. During the war, when meat was still available, the family doctor had advised him to eat mutton regularly and a "mutton lady" delivered mutton to the house each week. One day, the woman showed up in a state of high agitation and begged my parents to hide a Jewish girl in great danger and as soon as possible. Mother was instantly game, but my father smelled a rat. There was that SS man across the street and in a requisitioned house nearby lived a *Wehrmacht* General. My parents argued all night. Mother claimed it was the only argument they ever had. When the dawn came, father had prevailed: the girl would not be hidden. Mother would not forgive him until a few days after the war. The first paper published in our town had a story about the "mutton lady." Turned out she worked for the Gestapo as a *provocateur*, seeking out families likely to hide Jews. The *Binnenlandse Strijdkrachten*, former resistance units temporarily in charge of public order, hanged her from a tree. Summary justice, case closed, but if mother had won the day, my parents would have been interned, possibly killed, with the fate of my brother uncertain. I might not have been born at all, and that got my attention. We don't know whether the girl existed or was a figment of the trap, but I now knew that my very existence had been a matter of chance. I was a very lucky bastard and I would remember.

This episode underscored the providential quirkiness of war. It certainly was not the good show I had been sorry to have missed a few years younger. More importantly, it was the genesis of my attention, perhaps even obligation, to the fate of Jews, the canaries in the mine-shaft of our time, stretching back some two thousand years, a corner-stone of the weight World War II put on me.

Perspectives on the emergence of the Holocaust as a major post-war theme are remarkably consistent about those elements that brought to this theme prominence, instead of silence. Even more remarkable is the absence of hard data to support these perspectives. In Peter Novick's *The Holocaust in American Life* we are told that the cold war and, in that context, the redemption of the renewed West German democracy, had a repressive effect on Holocaust memorization and study. Then we find a varying set of circumstances that brought about change: the Eichmann trial that opened the 1960s,[8] the 1967 six-day war, the Yom Kippur war of 1973 (see note 3) brought a renewed sense of Jewish vul-nerability, as well as the use of the Holocaust as a counterweight against the centrifugal pressures of assimilation among Jewry, especially in America. There are two points to be made about this issue.

First, the supposed silence about the Holocaust during the fifties and sixties is an artifact. Think of the appearance of the *Diary* of Anne Frank, the works of Poliakov, Hilberg, Arendt, Frankl, Wiesel, and films on broader war topics such as *Judgment at Nuremberg* and *Night and Fog*. Arguably, as Novick contends, all these efforts may have had little effect.

The second point is that growing Holocaust awareness may not primarily be event driven. Steve Paulsson and others contend that growing interest in the Holocaust reflected the emergence of broader societal themes such as the anti-racism of the Civil Rights movement in the 1960s, the concern with wartime atrocities rekindled by the Vietnam War and movement, and the renewal of anti-fascism in the political radicalization of this era in the sixties and seventies.

I am of the view that those who place the growth in attention to the Holocaust within changes in society's consciousness hold a more defensible position than those who see this attention evolving from a series of external catalysts, the kind of events just noted. To be succinct: notions that the Holocaust grew in prominence because of such mile-stones as Israel's wars suffer from a fundamental fallacy: *post hoc, propter hoc*. If we really want to know what drew hundreds of scholars to this field, one would have to ask them. Nobody has done so yet. I believe that the social milieu, childhood experiences, and the *Zeitgeist* of one's era weave a much more convincing tapestry than any particular series of historical punctuations.

The story about that Jewish girl who needed a hiding place was certainly fundamental to the centrality of the Holocaust in my thinking about the war and on my later views on broader questions of persecution, up to and including genocide.

There was another central experience in my childhood that would matter a great deal. A boy moved into my neighborhood and my class when I was around six years old. We became fast friends and we are still so close that we can finish each other's sentences—if one of us would allow the other just to finish any at all, that is.

Over the years, Jack and I became brothers truer than blood brothers. We share a whole set of personality traits. We are brass, restless, and opinionated. We are extrovert but in that odd way I have often recognized in other extroverts. We masquerade pain by humor and our true selves are almost never fully on display, although we think of ourselves as honest and authentic at all times – paragons of frankness. Truth is, we are staging an act. We are jesters, and it is fair to say that we can be pretty funny together. Admittedly, we can roll over the floor with laughter while nobody around us has the foggiest idea what is so funny. When together, we seem to undergo a metamorphosis. We fuse into one person, like identical twins, and we draw reckless energy from one another. We are probably unbearable to others when that happens, and quite a handful because, when together, we use no brakes. We read each other like no other. We are a piece of work, and that piece began to take shape when we were little lads.

We liked the same girls but, at that age, it is a joint sentiment, free of competition. We endlessly played soccer, one-on-one, each defending a brick. When darkness fell, our goodbyes went like this: *"Nou, krijg de koelere." "Jij ook, en de typhus!"* Having wished cholera and typhoid fever upon one another, we went home, knowing we were as thick as thieves. So my friend Jack appears and he happens to be Jewish. When we were little the only apparent difference was that, on Saturday, he went to *shul* and I did shopping for my mother. I could not understand anything about this Nazi ideology with antisemitism at its core: was Jack not my alter ego? Therein lays the genesis of wanting to know more about the Nazis. When you don't "get" something and you are a moderately bright, curious kid, you want to, and so Jack's friendship was the second, highly personal reason to learn more about the Holocaust.

Another, not too dissimilar, experience would happen in the *gymnasium*, high school. My first high school crush was Jewish. Her parents had been in Theresienstadt and Auschwitz. Roselien was cute. She had great eyes (like her mother whom I adored). She was smart (like her dad whose intellect awed me). She has a strong personality, the strongest among the girls in my class. She was quick as an athlete, and even quicker as a humorist. In that memorable phrase of Sting she could be "...all four seasons in one day." I was mesmerized by her moods, and clueless about dealing with the unpredictability of her affections – all emotional ones, mind you, because in those days there was no sex in high schools.

Ergo, my oldest and closest friends (Roselien and I are also still in close touch) were both Jewish and as a youngster I simply refused any notion that they were the proverbial "other." Later in life I would come to understand that philosemitism is racist. It is best just not to see Jews as others. I do that though it confuses people: on occasion a co-worker will wish me Happy New Year in September![9] At a 1991 Anne Frank exhibit we hosted, a Dutch survivor repeatedly asked me whether I was Jewish. I finally threw in the towel and fibbed "yes." "Funny," she said, "You don't *look* Jewish."

Jack, his dad, Max, and I went to all the home games of Ajax, the Amsterdam soccer team which had periods of glory as a European powerhouse in the 1970s and 1990s. Though the myth that Ajax was a "Jewish" club has been dismantled by Simon Kuper, a fine soccer writer, it certainly felt Jewish in my day when there were such Jewish players as Sjaak Swart, Mr. Ajax, a furious winger, and Bennie Muller, a midfield assassin. Most importantly, a row ahead of me sat a season ticket holder who was rumored to have flown Eichmann out of Argentina: a superhero.

Epistemologically, I agree with Ian Buruma who considers the most important event during our adolescence to be the Dutch coverage of Case 40/61, the Eichmann trial (see note 8), by Harry Mulisch, the son of a Jewish mother and an Austrian Nazi collaborator and the extraordinary writer of *The Discovery of Heaven* and many other books that guided my life. His book on the trial, *De Zaak 40/61*, was recently published in translation by the University of Pennsylvania Press. My Dutch copy hangs on threads as I read and re-read it many times, not with a "certain pornographic *frisson*" with which Buruma admits to reading this literature but because Mulisch dispensed with the idea of "good" and "wrong" in this book and in much of his other writing, and in a way I thought infinitely better than Arendt's treatment of the same trial. I did a big project on the trial in school—possibly in part to impress Roselien—and I began to see what we were all capable of so that we had better watch what we do in life and avoid any situation where we might be tempted by the demons within (slipping regularly during much drunken violence in early college life). I developed wariness about the powerful attraction of all closed worldviews and ideologies, not just fascism and communism. The French call it *La puissance d'une idée en marche*: we know the road to hell is clearly paved with good intentions. Those who have read Graham Greene's *The Quiet American* may have a sense of this. For those opposed to the salvation of the marching drummer, or those who are the object of ideated wrath, there is often only death: millions die because terror is not a side effect but the central core of utopia; more about this point later.

Once a university student in 1964 I realized that with any kind of sensitivity to a city's landscape (and I had briefly flirted with architecture as a possible major) you cannot walk through Amsterdam without confronting the empty holes left by the decimation of the Jews. The Jewish quarter? Gone. Synagogues? Converted to musea. I had fraternity brothers living in a student dorm next to the Anne Frank House. Friends from my days as a tour guide at the Amstel Brewery (nice student job, that) bought *Eik en Linde*, a bar adjacent to the *Hollandse Schouwburg*, the Dutch Theater where Jews were held before the train transports to transit camp Westerbork and then to Auschwitz, Sobibor, Bergen Belsen and other death camps. I spent a lot of time in my friend Pieter Lakeman's apartment on the *Plantage Kerklaan*, which backed up to the *Schouwburg*, too.

In brief, the war still imposed itself on the present and the present drew in the war; in my case, the Holocaust took on a role more central and perhaps earlier than among my contemporaries.

Dealing with that centrality became a weight but also cast its shadows forward. How we, the lucky ones who had avoided the war, would deal with our lives was the unspoken question raised by our parents. We were not the children of survivors or perpetrators with their own traumas that would enter post-Holocaust literature over time, but we were a post-war generation that felt a parental expectation, imagined or not, that we were to do something with our lives.

Amsterdam

As we began to ponder the question of what to do with our lives, Dutch society faced the 1960s. Baby boomers entered universities in record numbers but the universities did not have the staff or cultural capacity to absorb them. The number of faculty did not keep pace with the sudden flood of students. Lecture classes ran into the hundreds and students faced a non-plussed cohort of faculty out of touch with their rapidly radicalizing charges. Like our compatriots in France and Germany, the "68er" generation was whipping up the winds of a generational storm against the repressive regent mentality of the political elite that had its formative days in pre-war norms, values, and party structures.

Moreover, the faculty still advanced through research. Teaching prowess was given short shrift but professorial authority could no longer protect them as before. Society's deference to authority was declining: we no longer deferred to faculty, though we feared their grading of exams. Clearly, perhaps through no fault of their own, their training had left them woefully unprepared for the pedagogical challenges of rapid university expansion. Their response was unimaginative. I am not sure they realized a sea change was under way. At university, we talked about mind over matter: faculty did not mind and we did not matter.

Retention rates were awful as was progression toward degree completion. Sometimes it seemed that only the dreaded hammer of the draft got students to make any progress at all. The blowback of first year exam results was the departure of a good third of freshmen from the *subfaculteit* A of the University of Amsterdam where I had embarked on a political science degree.

Students felt alienated, and the pinkish hue of Marxism rapidly enveloped growing majorities of my alma mater, as was the case elsewhere. My last name did not help in this environment. Guilt by (name) association with the pre-war PM strong man Colijn was not a good thing. I wonder whether my experience would have been different at the Christian *Vrije Universiteit* where Colijn had been chairman of the Trustees, but the point is moot because the *Vrije* did not have my major.

The American sixties were driven by the Vietnam War, but that war arguably played a lesser, though not unimportant, role in The Netherlands. The war was overshadowed by trouble in the universities and trouble with the royals. After an earlier scandal surrounding the Queen and a faith healer, Greet Hofmans, brought in to help with the serious sight impairment of Princess Christina, Beatrix, the crown princess, fell in love with a young German diplomat, Claus von Amsberg who had served in the Hitler Youth ("Who hadn't?" was not a relevant question in our mind). Then, with the stubbornness of her grandmother, she insisted the marriage take place in left-wing Amsterdam, the least royalist city of all but the Dutch capitol (a bit unusual, the seat of government is in The Hague). Riots broke out not only between students, other radicals such as the anarchist and often playful *Provos* and the police but also with off-duty Marines stationed at the nearby navy base in Den Helder, mostly lower class kids who did not mind kicking some high IQ ass; they descended upon the city like locusts.

The wedding took place with teargas drifting over the city. I was head bartender at the Lido, a bar with excellent music each night, for example, the Louis van Dijk trio, Rita Reys, or Kabani, a student orchestra that played gypsy music. The Lido was at the *Leidseplein* in the middle of town. A buddy and I walked into the chaos after work and were immediately arrested, thrown in a paddy wagon and driven to the police riding stable where hundred of other students were sitting in a rink full of shit, singing *Sinterklaas* (Santa Claus) songs to pass the night. We got out because my manager at the Lido was a student who happened to be a reserve officer and a big toff. He drove to police headquarters, threw names around to show he was well connected, and we left with an apologetic handshake of the chief of police, named Koppejan—Head John, and indeed he was.

I was very interested in politics but I detested the woolly nonsense spouted by the hard left in the student union. It lacked all nuance, and it was overwrought with a feverish silliness, such as the proposal that the university be run on the one man, one vote principle, giving equal weight to a janitor and a prof. In fact, we were so disgusted with the ideologically mindless herd mentality around us, that my fraternity brother Pieter Lakeman, later a scourge—like Ralph Nader—of fiddling corporations and politicians, started a new student party, *Het Algemeen Non-Politiek Studentenbelang*. It was to be a non-political student interest group, getting us what we really needed, a university that worked, a rational student grant system (the Marxists wanted student wages), restaurant, theater, and travel discounts, and cheaper beer, natch. We got a handful of seats but the times were not only changing, they were against us.

There was great irony in this. Hard left leaders later became part of the establishment, this one an alderman in Amsterdam, that one running a large institute at the university. Pieter remained the quintessential outsider, ever more prominent, such as by taking on the business practices of PM Ruud Lubbers in one of his bestsellers, but always against the grain. The Netherlands shifted to the right in the 1980s and 1990s as America did under Reagan and England under Thatcher, but Pieter's views did not. Always quite conservative, he was in final analysis more anti-establishment than any of his contemporary Red Rudies. He is more true to the 1960s than most because his emperors never have clothes: a muckraker to the core.

I have a main regret about those days. A leading moderate and eminent scholar, Hans Daudt, a fellow who could actually teach, too, got into a conflict with the more radical faculty. He should have received support from us but he never got it: student-faculty relations were such that, from our perspective, a faculty conflict was "a plague on both your houses." The matter eventually came to a head and Daudt left for the University of Leiden, more congenial to his talent and moderation. By that time, I had left for doctoral work in America.

The university had been occupied by students, and I had wasted a few years being at the margins of a crumbling system. I worked to be less financially dependent on mother so that I did not have to account for any bad exam results. As noted, I led tours at the Amstel Brewery; I tended bar; I had my head shaven again after hazing, to be the cover model on *Toeten en Blazen: Handboek voor Versierders*, a funny book on getting girls (it sold well), and I was an extra in the television series *Maigret*, opposite the great actor Ko van Dijk. For twenty-five guilders

I would jump, fully dressed, into the smelly Amstel River—anything for a buck. I ran a student hotel in London one year. I partied hard. I took close to a year off to organize the Gala Ball that culminated the *lustrum*, the anniversary of the *Amsterdams Studenten Corps*—a mostly non-Marxist old boys' club that was the umbrella of some twenty hard drinking, hard rowing, and hard womanizing fraternities, though some had the literary pretensions of a Bloomsbury set. The gala featured nine bands and a circus and my bodyguard was Wim Ruska, a world champ in martial arts. These were heady days but it was time to move on: America beckoned. I managed to pass my *kandidaat* orals (BA exams), with distinction (to the surprise of all) and then left.

What had I learned about living a life in those undergraduate days? Not much, one would think. I had acquired certain skills, running large events, running a business, supervising people, honing my French and German on brewery tours, but from a point of intellectual or moral growth, the university itself had been a bit of a waste. I learned more outside of the lecture halls than I ever did at university, debating for nights at the time with Pieter and other fraternity brothers, living under the cultural pulse of Amsterdam, being in the middle of the music and theater scene, reading anywhere from five to ten newspapers at the reading table in the *Hotel Americain* opposite the Lido, and always reading tons more literature than textbooks. Swimming against the hard left tide reinforced my wariness about closed ideological systems. Going against the grain of the times, questioning conventional wisdom among my peers, charting a contrarian intellectual path, not becoming a joiner (certainly not of majorities, of political masses) seemed to fit a self-reliant, mildly narcissistic personality, and to that extent these years perhaps served their purpose after all.

Philadelphia

Originally, I was bound for America for a primary reason other than graduate work—love.

I had fallen for a Philadelphia girl who was in Amsterdam under the aegis of Syracuse University. We went to London to run a hotel, and I visited Philadelphia and Syracuse in December 1968. We got engaged. Nancy was Jewish. I still refused to see Jews as the proverbial other: it must have been a nightmare for those who worry about assimilation.

The engagement did not last but when it was over there was little point in staying at the University of Amsterdam. The university continued to be a mess and the faculty conflicts raged. I wanted to specialize in International Relations and an American Ph.D. made sense. While still with Nancy, I had applied to several universities, Yale, Penn, American, among others, but Temple made a generous offer and, as I was going to be on my own, finances were going to matter a great deal, so Temple it was and off I went (after a glorious farewell party that lasted more than twenty-four hours; that kind of stuff needs doing right).

The first years in America were challenging. There were minor frustrations in dealing with banks, the phone company, a driver's license, visa stipulations, learning American English, and some minor cultural adjustments thrown in for good order. They were mostly just the hassles faced in any new country. There was the business of the landscape of a vast university and a higher education system much different from what I knew: accessible faculty, dinners at their homes, small seminars. There was my teaching fellowship, teaching undergraduates whose analogies escaped me. I trust they thought me pretty exotic, but humor goes a long way.

World War II and the Netherlands were no longer part of my day-to-day life although, the day Ajax won its first Europe Cup at Wembley, I got a Dutch international directory operator to hold the phone next to the radio. No charge for two hours of transatlantic bliss.

World War II receded because America now had a new, ugly conflict on its hand: the Vietnam War was tearing at its fabric. As a guest on a student visa I did not take much part in the campus unrest surrounding the war. Like Muhammad Ali, I had no *dawg* in the fight, and under NATO and other regulations I could not be drafted, again. Whatever I thought of the war, the draft was not my problem. In Amsterdam I had learned that the false currency of many political demonstrations is a sense of moral superiority. I knew many marchers also found "demos" a good way to meet "chicks," but I knew a museum is a better stomping ground: more interesting women and no teargas. I mostly just observed and listened to the war's protagonists, my faculty, student leaders, and firebrands like Angela Davis.

At Temple, I was learning the cutting edge in International Relations, Comparative Politics, and Political Behavior against a backdrop of knowing woefully little about America's constitutional roots, its federalism, and their evolution over time—I was busy.

Despite Temple's generosity there was not much time for student or other politics because I was at the bottom of the economic ladder. My finances were precarious, marginal enough that I regularly found myself at a midtown eatery, Horn and Hardart's. You got a roll, loaded up on condiments and presto, you had a semblance of a meal. Summers I worked. I started in a wholesale hat company, scraping fungus off water-logged hats that would be sold as new to Gimbels and Macy's. I did translations. I ran a breakfast joint, flipping eggs and burning toast. I sold encyclopedias door-to-door, cold calls of course, and was shot at in a Delaware development, and bitten by a dog, another time.

I worked the night shift as a switchboard operator/manager at International House where you might check in an Aussie girl, comatose with jet lag and fatigue who would ask: "Can you knock me up at eight in the morning?" Funny colloquialisms were everywhere in I-House, a residence of foreign and American students that became my world. There was the legendary promiscuity of its social life but more importantly it was a brainy neighborhood. You *had* to be a smart cookie to get into American graduate school from Bangladesh, Eritrea, or the West Bank: we occupied a rare transnational space among some of the most brilliant and sexiest people alive. The parochial values we brought with us were challenged in our musings about the America wherein we found ourselves. Playing de Tocqueville helped us understand where we were but also where we came from. The diversity among the students also gave us a sophisticated, nuanced view of the world abroad. When the Shah was ousted, we had first row seats as Iranian residents violently argued with each other, split three ways among Shah supporters, lefties, and the religious supporters of the new regime who were not called fundamentalist—as yet.

Where else in the world could you debate the Middle East with a French MBA student, two students of the legendary architect Louis Kahn, one Iraqi and the other Egyptian, and a Polish Jew who grew up in Israel and studied film at Annenberg? On the cusp of one's home and American culture, and under a kaleidoscope of the cultures of friends, we wanderers became very cosmopolitan, post-modern, if not yet fully post-national, subtle in our thinking, learning to detect thought patterns and manners in others, valuable skills much beyond the international bonhomie I had learned at the brewery. (Years later, when the first Gulf war broke out in 1991, I phoned Israeli friends who were huddled in a basement as Saddam's Scud missiles dropped; then my Egyptian friend, now in Jeddah who was flying his family out but was staying because of the dogs, and finally my Iraqi buddy who had just quit a good job in Princeton, in order to take one in Kuwait which now was not going to happen: he would open an art gallery in old Philadelphia later. It was a strange opening day of Gulf War I).

I was working on a dissertation about the influence of Benelux, an early transnational customs union (now Benelux Economic Union), on what was still called the European Economic Community. I had a fine dissertation supervisor, Lynn Miller, who had studied under Richard Falk and who drew new windows on possible global order. For the first time, there was synergy between my university life and life outside. My scope became increasingly transnational and the Philadelphia years were a good basis for a future I did not yet know. I later realized that the Philadelphia days had expanded my horizons to great benefit.

Pomona: the weight returns

Near the end of my Ph.D. and, therefore, of my student visa, I had to decide what to do next. I thought I would take the attaché exam with an eye on joining the Dutch Foreign Service. Then a place named Stockton College called my department at Temple. They needed a visiting lecturer for a year. At the time, many of my friends would graduate in May, do the grand tour in an old VW bus, and then return to Europe or Asia. Well, the academic year would end next May so that would work. I never went home, and I trust the Grand Canyon will be there when I come: the job became permanent, and a few years later I was tenured before becoming chair of Social and Behavioral Sciences. Stockton was a wonderful college to begin a career. One faced the typical challenges of developing a course repertory, a bit of "publish or perish," and negotiating yet another institutional landscape but it really was remarkably easy. The college was just five years old when I joined. I did not need to uncover hidden traditions that would have to be found and mastered (as in old European universities) at a point when you have little idea what you are doing. Nobody else seemed to know what to do either. Groomed by the sixties, we figured it out together in the absence of any hierarchy of rank or formality. Plus, we were building a college from scratch, a rare opportunity in academe. I got married in 1986. When you, finally, fall into the kind of love that leads to marriage, you are in a dimension that does not exist in physics. You are in a bottomless, all-encompassing crevice that wraps all around you, below you, next to you, and above you, yet you are flying miles high. Sarah is not Jewish so that buried the "proverbial other" business. It was clearly better to marry without even a tinge of that political agenda of past romances when I always seemed to fall in love while also wanting to prove that Jew plus non-Jew could "work." To marry for reasons of romance only is a self-evident truth I learned rather late! We took a sabbatical at the University of Warwick where I was a visiting fellow in the departments of politics and in international relations and Sarah got her M.A. We got a child, Cory, and I became a dean—all fine, happy events.

Then a minor administrative decision jolted my intellectual life for decades to come. The college president, Vera King Farris, and some Jewish leaders in the community decided to start a Holocaust Resource Center and she put it in my shop. In the blink of an eye, the weight was back, after years of hibernation, and back with a vengeance. World War II and the Holocaust began to drive my professional life. I had to ramp up in a hurry. The logical point of entry was to read first about what had happened in Dutch society and historiography since I left and then take on the broader canvas. I got a lot of help along the way. The next few pages, therefore, contain a parade of scholars. Name-dropping is annoying but here simply acknowledges the debts of a political scientist who arrived at serious work on genocide later than many historians.

As early as 1955 the Dutch government, in response to a proposal of the war documentation institute, the *Rijksinstituut voor Oorlogsdocumentatie* (RIOD), had given the historian Lou de Jong the task to write a multi-volume history on the Kingdom of the Netherlands in the Second World War. The first volume appeared in 1969. It would take thirty years to complete the study. It spanned the pre-war, war, and post-war years, and also covered the overseas territories, Surinam, the Dutch Antilles, the Dutch East Indies, and after the colonial period ended, what became known as Indonesia. It was a massive undertaking, impassively balanced, read by tens of thousands.

The vast scope of de Jong's work made him a legitimate arbiter of who and what had been good or "*fout*" during the war. In addition to the scholarly work, he was a regular on radio and television. That public role had its complications. Sitting in judgment on the facts, de Jong was soft on several political notables such as the NATO Secretary-General Joseph Luns who had been a member of the Dutch National Socialist Party (NSB) from 1933 to 1936. He was also soft on Jan de Quay who eventually became prime minister in 1959, in the early years of the war one of the leaders of a new political movement, the *Nederlandse Unie* (Dutch Union), organized to accommodate the new realities of German occupation. The *Unie* was short-lived. De Quay fell out with the Germans, but it was a dubious episode. It is difficult to trace de Jong's reticence in these cases. Perhaps the Kingdom's official chronicler decided that there were limits to his political discretion. Perhaps the 1950s political climate had not yet sufficiently reassessed the war, allowing someone like de Quay to rise to the premiership. Two decades later, de Jong was less forgiving in 1978 to another parliamentarian, Protestant (ARP) party leader, Wim Aantjes: his career would come to an immediate end when it was reported that he had joined the *Waffen* SS (in fact, he had joined the Dutch SS, but the damage was done). The chicken or egg question is: Had de Jong's views evolved or was Aantjes a victim of the more critical war reassessment now under way in the Netherlands?

De Jong was not the only one taking on the Holocaust. In 1968 another prominent historian, Jacques Presser, published a monumental and passionate indictment of the Dutch role in the Holocaust, *De Ondergang* (The Destruction). He was harshly critical of the indifference of the "bystanders," of the complicity of Dutch authorities in the deportations, and of the role of the Jewish Council and its leadership. The book appeared in Britain in 1969 as *Ashes in the Wind* and was published in the United States as *The Destruction of Dutch Jewry.* Presser's book became a bestseller. It raised the kind of questions that had not been asked before, focusing on a key issue of the war: the destruction of Dutch Jews had been, in essayist Ido de Haan's summation, "a crime against a group of Dutch citizens, committed by Germans, with the knowledge and collaboration of the Dutch."

Clearly a reassessment was under way. Years later, that assessment took an even blunter tone. Judith Miller, in *One by One by One*, and Sylvain Ephimenco, in *Hollandse Kost* (Dutch Fare), argued that the Dutch had engaged in a collective public relations campaign by using

Anne Frank's *Diary* to pretend that quite a number of Jews had been helped in hiding and that most of the Dutch population had resisted in one way or another. Those views were a bit over the top but the self-image of the Dutch lay in shatters. Survivors, often child survivors, were writing their memoirs and novels, for example, Gerhard Durlacher (*The Search, Stripes in the Sky,* and *Drowning: Growing up in the Third Reich*) and Marga Minco (*The Glass Bridge* and *Bitter Herbs*): the victims were silent no more.

In the 1990s, Nanda van der Zee wrote an indictment even stronger than Presser in *Om erger te voorkomen* (To avoid worse). She debunked the myth of Dutch tolerance. This myth was created by the grateful praises of just a few intellectuals who had found refuge in Holland, Voltaire among others. She also debunked the myth of Dutch heroism. Sure, the majority of the approximately 25,000 Jews who went into hiding between 1940 and 1945 were saved and that could not have happened but for the assistance of thousands of Dutch citizens. But such assistance and the resistance it symbolized was even more remarkable because of the failure of the Dutch elite after the flight of Queen Wilhelmina to London in May 1940.[10]

Van der Zee's book took a tack quite different from another highly controversial book that appeared around the same time, Daniel Goldhagen's *Hitler's Willing Executioners.* In Goldhagen's view, the Holocaust resulted from virulent antisemitism across Germany and virtually all Germans were culpable. Van der Zee, and others such as Dienke Hondius, did not find such levels of antisemitism in the Netherlands. She put the blame squarely on the authorities, who, at every step of the way, collaborated with the Germans: in a society still quite hierarchical and deferential to authority, it was the elite that failed to exercise moral leadership.

We had come a long way since Raul Hilberg's *The Destruction of the European Jews* (1967), one of the first landmark studies in the field. Hilberg cited certain incontrovertible factors to explain the disproportionate number of Jewish victims in the Netherlands. Hilberg had noted the location of the Netherlands, which prevented easy escape and several borders to be crossed before the relative safety of Spain, Portugal, and eventually England. He wrote about the Dutch topography, the absence of vast forests that had provided hiding places to Jewish and other partisans in Poland, for example, and he noted the deadly accurate population registry in which each Jew was easily traced. He had noted the complicity of the civil service bureaucracy, the municipal councils, police, and postal service, too.

Van der Zee, however, put culpability at a perch dramatically higher than Hilberg, de Jong, or even Presser. Queen Wilhelmina herself had essentially ignored the fate of the Jews as had her government-in-exile. The civil service just took its cue and obeyed the Nazis from A to Z. Several sacred cows were slain at once. She demolished the image of Wilhelmina as "mother of the resistance" by concluding that the Queen had not lifted a finger for the Jews before, during, and after the war, destroyed several myths in the Dutch self-imagery about their role in the war, and, last but not least, took on de Jong who had been much more muted about the government-in-exile whose London exile he had shared, working for Dutch radio. Compared to, say, the Danes—from King Christian X and the political leaders to the common rescuers, van der Zee struck a nail in the coffin of the myth of the good, tolerant, and heroic Dutch.

There are other realities that debunk that myth. The archives of the special war tribunals (*Centraal Archief Bijzondere Rechtspraak*) contain some 760,000 files of those whose wartime behavior had been suspect or worse. Granted, some of these files just contain an allegation by a neighbor, but other files include the complete membership of the NSB, SS volunteers, war profiteers, and those who turned in Jews for money. The Dutch mid-war population was 9.3 million so that the number of files represents some ten percent of the adult population. Some 64,000 were ultimately convicted, but that figure did not include the Dutch police that had rounded up Jews, often with not a German in sight. The post-war government had made a judgment that the persecution of the overwhelming majority of the police would have left the country virtually stripped of any law enforcement.

In an ironic twist, when she wrote her book, Nanda van der Zee was married to a muckraker we already met: Pieter Lakeman. His field is econometrics; it certainly was not his book. But he loved it all the same. His emperors have no clothes. Her Queen had none either.

The development of Dutch historiography on the Holocaust was in and by itself insufficient for what needed to be known. With responsibility for the Holocaust Resource Center and for a curriculum with a growing number of undergraduate Holocaust (and later genocide) courses, a broader take on the field was needed not only in terms of administrative responsibility but to buttress research.

Under tutelage of an eminent Israeli Holocaust scholar, Yehuda Bauer, whom we hired several times as distinguished visiting professor in a newly created chair in Holocaust studies which rotated each year, we began to see clarity on the field's epistemological controversies, such as the functionalism-intentionalism debate. Was there a grand design that led, in fairly linear fashion, from *Mein Kampf* to Auschwitz, or had it been a helter skelter, much more opportunist path, pending on the development of the war itself? It is clear that options other than extermination, for example, the deportation of Jews to destinations as diverse as Madagascar and Siberia still cropped up well after the war had started. It was also clear that the Holocaust had taken place with far less than the lockstep organizational tightness of command one expects in a totalitarian regime. Bauer's guidance was a great influence and not only on us. His views underpin parts dealing with the Holocaust in Ian Kershaw's tour de force, *Hitler 1936-1945 Nemesis*. I know many others indebted to Bauer.

Among new national reinterpretations, there was the American question whether Roosevelt could have done more during the years prior to the war despite immigration quota (very probably: one only had to think of the tragedy of the *SS St. Louis* whose passengers could have disembarked *somewhere* in the Caribbean with a bit of US jawboning) and after the war had begun, for instance, by bombing the death camps (much less likely). France, where most resistance fighters appeared to have joined very late (or after the war as the pundits had it), faced the long tribulation in coming to a honest reckoning of the role of the Vichy government. On France, I learned a lot from the work of Michael Marrus. Austria was still in denial in its presumption of a nation victimized, well through the days after UN Secretary General Kurt Waldheim's role in rounding up Jews had been exposed. A fierce debate took place in Germany where historians were battling the so-called *Historikerstreit*, which centered on the question: should the Holocaust be looked at in and by itself, or should it be seen in the context of Stalin's crimes and thereby contextualized in a way that mitigated Nazi crimes?

The issue that raised the most furor was the uniqueness debate, the argument whether or not the Holocaust had been so exceptional in scope, single-minded intent, and success that it was qualitatively different from *any* other pre-or post-war genocides, in a class by itself, the single plumb line against which all genocide should be measured. In the eyes of uniqueness proponents such as Steven Katz other genocides invariably fell short. Such judgment marred his monumental work. The debate was not only passionate but quite awful, with charges of racism flying back and forth. Irrespective of the question whether the Holocaust should be the plumb line, it had better be understood that there is no pyramid in suffering, no hierarchy in pain. To organize reality in ways that suggest otherwise is, frankly, a pornographic effrontery.

Thankfully, today the plumb line debate does not take the centrality it once had. There has been growing recognition of other victims exterminated by the Nazis, and there is more acknowledgment of atrocities such as the Armenian genocide and the genocide of Native Americans. Moreover, some countries are re-examining their colonial eras and concomitant carnage. We are sobered in the knowledge that the phrase "Never again" increasingly rings hollow as the last century came to a close and the new century began with genocide continuing.[11] Rwanda, Cambodia, the Sudan are among dozens of genocides that occupy scholars and activists today.

Holocaust study has appropriately evolved into comparative genocide study under the leadership of Helen Fein, Henry Huttenbach, and dozens of other genocide scholars whose work is organized in associations, presented in a burgeoning conference circuit, published in such journals as the *Journal of Genocide Research,* and, with an eye on future genocide prevention, supported by the government of Sweden. Whenever comparative work is done in a new field, paradigmatic questions arise and those questions are the cutting edge of genocide studies in our time.

There is another point to be made about keeping the academic reins firmly on the currency of comparative genocide study. Bangladesh, Cambodia, East Timor, Sudan: the public attends to atrocities and massacres *ad seriatim.* Often compassion fatigue sets in. Each successive genocide covers people's memory of the previous one. When we say "six million" for example, we invariably refer to Jewish victims of the Nazis, but not to the six million that perished between 1942 and 1944 in a man-made famine in Bangladesh. Milan Kundera wrote in *The Book of Laughter and Forgetting* about people's incapacity to deal with the serialization of memory. Each successive genocide rolls over the previous one "and so on and so forth until ultimately everyone lets everything be forgotten." It is our job to be sure it is not.

Another important facet of the journey was a reassessment of Germans as I got to know more post-war contemporaries. My friend Roselien had startled me in the early 1990s when she said that she liked Germans and found them among the most interesting of our fellow Europeans. For a child of survivors, it was a surprising statement, yet I had begun to move in the same way, certainly with respect to young Germans (old ones without an arm or a leg are another matter). I had met a good number of Germans in graduate school and did not hold them responsible for the sins of the fathers. In 1991, at a college sponsored conference on the Netherlands and the Holocaust, I met a German who would have a lot to do with that reassessment and who was to become an associate and close friend, Gottfried Wagner, the great-grandson of Richard, Hitler's muse. Richard Wagner's radical and vitriolic antisemitic writings and stage works are at the core of Hitler's beliefs, a legacy that Gottfried would battle all his life.

Gottfried had an extraordinary youth. Growing up on the grounds of the Bayreuth Festival where his father was *Intendant* (manager), he was confronted at a very young age with the Wagners' intimate ties to Hitler. In school, he was stunned by film reels showing Nazi atrocities. He found a film reel in the sidecar of his father's motorcycle that documented his grandmother, his father, and his uncle happily hosting Hitler, known as Uncle Wolf, who had special accommodations on the Festival site. Questioning his father about all this, he was met with silence. The old man was carefully repositioning himself in the new, neo-liberal (West) Germany, and silence, repression, and denial were his best weapons. His grandmother, Winifred, was less squeamish. She was an unreconstructed Nazi who purportedly had given Hitler the paper to start writing *Mein Kampf* when he was in prison. There was also the story he had proposed to her when she became a widow. However, grandmother dismissed any questions by her grandson about these matters as propaganda by New York Jews. My weight was next to nothing compared to his. He had rebelled. He dissertation centered on Kurt Weill and Brecht, a nice act of defiance.[12] He fled the malodorous atmosphere of Bayreuth, got married and divorced, got married again to a beautiful Italian, Teresina, and moved to Italy. A bit later they adopted a Romanian boy, aptly named Eugenio. Gottfried had become the white sheep in the black Wagner family. We had endless talks as he worked on his book on the Wagners, *Wer nicht mit dem Wolf heult,* and I helped fix up a dreadful UK version for the American edition entitled *Twilight of the Wagners: The Unveiling of a Family's Legacy.*

I met other German scholars, such as Mathias Heyl and Lars Rensman, a bit younger than Gottfried and I, who were doing fine work (and I have co-authored some work with a brilliant Belgian theologian, Didier Pollefeyt, who is of the same generation). We hosted *gymnasium* high school students from the small town of Dinslaken near the Dutch border who put an exhibition together on the fate of their town's Jews in which a survivor now in New Jersey, Fred Spiegel, played a large role. They visited the College right after 9/11. This third generation is simply impressive. Interestingly enough many Germans deal more honestly with the Holocaust than most Europeans.

Gatherings among my own, the so-called second generation, were an important part of the journey. Gottfried writes and lectures with our mutual friend Abraham Peck, born in a displaced person (DP) camp to Holocaust survivors. Their dialogue is beneficial to all of us.

Another visiting distinguished Holocaust professor, the Israeli psychologist Dan Bar-On, added further dimensions to this work. Confronted with the trauma and unresolved psychological issues among the sons and daughters of survivors he had the simple idea to bring them together with children of perpetrators in the hope that, through mutual story telling, some personal healing and mutual understanding could be achieved with, just possibly, beneficial effects on situations of ongoing conflict. He got involved in several projects with Israelis and Palestinians along these lines and also with second generation Jews and Germans. In a subsequent phase we helped host a week-long conference not only with Jews and Palestinians, and Jews and Germans, but also with Irish participants on both sides of that conflict, and South Africans who had been on both sides of the Apartheid struggle. There were some tough *hombres* at that conference, folks who had served lengthy sentences because of their activities. It was a memorable week, with a depth of raw emotion that words cannot easily capture. Among the participants was Martin Bormann, the son of perhaps the second most powerful man in Hitler Germany, and Hitler's godson. The weight of his yoke was barely imaginable. He had found solace, until 1971, in the priesthood: extraordinary.[13]

Coda

Let us now turn to the second part of this book, my father's memoirs. As noted in the introduction, his stories are transcribed without changes, except for an occasional explanatory note inserted with parentheses, and his writing in English—as opposed to American English—is left untouched as well.

His memoirs make reference to the destruction of Dutch Jewry, but they do not center on this tragedy. Instead, they focus on the realities of occupation for the non-Jewish population, for example, on the constant fear among men of deportation and forced labor, on the issue of food (a near obsession during the last days of the war), on the day-to-day challenges under Nazi occupation, and on the mental and physical deprivations of people who are not free.

Why is the concurrent destruction of Dutch Jewry not more prominent? Most observers would agree that the destruction followed a nefarious, incremental path, intended to separate the non-Jewish majority from the unfolding tragedy by first segregating the Jews, for example, by firing them from the civil service, followed by physical isolation in a ghetto, then transportation (mostly to transit camp Westerbork first), followed by deportation east, to the death camps and the final chapter—extermination. As the timeline at the end of this book shows, the isolation of Jews from Dutch society was carefully orchestrated to avoid sympathy and/or resistance among the Dutch population at large: it was a lethal campaign of remarkable success, with the actual genocide taking place elsewhere.

At any rate, let us now find out what the war and the German occupation were like for my family.

PART TWO

The Second Great War–Looking Backward

The Second Great War— Looking Backward

1940-1945

Was there ever a time in which so many plans that were made had to be abandoned as in the five years of the second Great War? Amongst many other things it has been my intention for ever so long to make short notes of important events, to fill a map with newspaper cuttings, to collect data for a survey of these memorable days.

The excellent plan was never carried out. The reason? There were many. The struggle of "to be" or "not to be" was at times so severe that it was absolutely impossible to find the spare moment for correspondence or mental activities of any kind—on other days the general outlook of things had become so oppressing that it was difficult to retain the optimism or keep up the right spirit to see the attractiveness of such work.

But last week a former pupil of mine dropped in and asked me if I would have a look at a short treatise of his which he had called: The postponed Liberation. Before the war it had been his custom to go to England every year in the summer holidays, where an uncle of his lived. He was looking forward to his next visit and expected to hear as soon as he had set foot on English soil again:

"And how did you manage to get through the war in Holland?" It might be useful to hand them these sheets then and say, "Well, have a look at this. These are my notes. I wrote down the most important things that happened to me and in our country from the invasion on the 6th of June 1944 until the time when the heavy burden of occupation was taken from us."

When he came with this request, I said: "Yes." We spent some time over corrections, I gave him some hints, suggested other chapters, advised him to omit irrelevant information in other places. And at the end the impetus this perusal of his experiences has given me was so strong that I said: "Now or never."

The following essay intends to give you some general idea of the whole period of the war. I go back further than my friend and shall begin on the 10th of May 1940. The date for us has about the same meaning as Sept. 1939 for you. This must be my introductory chapter. After that I shall resume the thread of my story on June 6th 1944, because everything that happened in between has been reduced to material of secondary importance. Besides it would make my notes too extensive and at the moment that I am writing down these words war is still going on – our rations are worse than they have ever been—it is still "perish or survive", but new hope is stirring our hearts: The Allies have crossed the river Ijssel—and even very pessimistic individuals, and I am one—seem to have good reason for the thought that our worst days are over.

The tenth of May

The 10th of May is for us, Dutchmen, about the same as September 1939 for you. Shall we ever forget this memorable day? At about half past three we were awakened by the whir of innumerable aircraft very high in the air. It was altogether different from the sound of our own aeroplanes starting at Soesterberg, the military flying ground only a few miles from the place were we lived. On getting out of bed we saw the planes—glittering flashes of light in the bright spring morning. For weeks we had been expecting a sudden break in the comparative quietness of our neutral state. And now that it had come, it fell upon us as if an enormous weight had been hurled down at us to wipe us out.

Uncanny, I think that is the word which most adequately describes what we felt when we saw the tiny specks floating past in Westerly direction. One of our neigbours, a staunch supporter of the National Socialist Movement in our country, and the only representative of Mussert's party in our street, was standing on the balcony of his house *(note: Anton*

Mussert, leader of the Dutch National Socialist Party, or N.S.B.)

In his black shirt—with folded arms—striking an attitude in accordance with the military character of these heralds of a new era. Presently his loud bass voice announced to us:

"Mere practice—nothing serious." Even at that early date these words didn't carry weight. We all knew that the days of peace were over for us.

Some boys who had not been satisfied with the spectacle as it was shown to us in all its grand and sinister impressiveness had cycled to Soesterberg, but they did not get so far. After they had witnessed two planes come down in a blaze, they returned to tell us that they had witnessed the first, light skirmishes between the invaders and our own defensive weapons.

At about seven o'clock we heard the queen over the wireless. Her voice did not show a tremor, but it was flat and colourless and seemed to reflect the mood of depression that had taken possession of all of us.

She gave the facts—sober and objective. A visit from the German ambassador at the Hague. Request to grant a free passage of the army of 'the Reich'—which had been politely, but firmly refused. Notation of our frontiers. Declaration of war from the Netherlands to Germany.

Proclamation of Her Majesty the Queen   *The Hague, 10th May 1940*

My People,

Although our country had observed a strict neutrality all these months and had no other intention than to keep up this attitude rigidly and consistently, during the past night the German army suddenly without the least warning made an attack on our territory. This notwithstanding the promise that the neutrality of our country should be respected as long as we maintained it ourselves.

I herewith put up a flaming protest against this unprecedented violation of good faith and the attack on what is considered to be decent among civilized nations.

I and my Government will do our duty also at this moment. You will do yours everywhere and in all circumstances, everyone in the place to which he has been appointed with great watchfulness and with that peace of mind and devotion which a stainless conscience gives.

Wilhemina

At the time our army had been mobilized for about half a year. From September 1939 onwards the tension at our frontiers had been so marked that all the measures that could be taken to defend our country had to be carried out. In consequence of this our little school had been depleted of two-thirds of its staff. The head, a reserve officer, had been summoned to take up his quarters in Muiden, one of the little villages in what we call Vesting Holland, the inner most and last resort of our defensive system, and my colleague had been sent to Groningen where his regiment had been sent to guard the Eastern frontier. For all we knew he might have fallen at that very hour as one of the early victims in this period of our active part in the Second Great War.

I was the only one left in charge. To school, or not to school, that was the question. I went—spoke with the heads of other schools and we decided to send the pupils home. It proved to have been the best plan, for when I came back, my wife had already been warned for evacuation in the late afternoon of the same day.

And at six o'clock we actually turned the key in the front door of our house. Queer thought is not it to close the door with the idea: you may never see the place again where you entered a new stage of life—a married man; where your son was born; where you lost a father—and where you had dropped off to sleep with the peaceful tinkling of the bell of the last train leisurely puffing away to Utrecht.

At seven o'clock we were at Baarn. In half an hour our train would be on its way to the North of West-Friesland which was considered to be a safer place for civilians. It was half past nine before the engine-driver got the signal for starting. And in those long hours of waiting the enemy planes were hovering over our heads, and we heard the anti-aircraft guns at Soesterberg barking in the distance. Fortunately we had not yet sunk so low that the word 'total warfare' had been invented. One dive of a chaser—one bomb of medium size and this story could not have been told.

In the dark we felt more at ease—and cold too. For it was a frightfully long journey. Now it was three o'clock a.m. before we were at our destination. The burgomaster of the little village that was to receive us had been informed of our coming at the last moment but his organizing power had made it possible to give us all some glasses of hot milk when we assembled in the old Protestant church. From the pulpit he read out the names of our hosts—and after another hour we lay down on the bare floor of a kind, but poor family who had been invited to open their door to us.

I said to my wife: "Is not it strange that only a few hours of war can work this miracle—everything may be lost, but here we are—safe and sound—quite prepared to make a new beginning if necessary."

From Invasion to Capitulation

Is this a short chapter because the less said about it the better? Must we really be ashamed that after five days our Commander-in-chief capitulated for the overwhelming masses of Germans?

Most of us did not know what he could have done else. Even where we were fully mobilized—as it was then understood, so no boys of 17, 16 and under that age as we saw later on and no greybeards as we have seen them since—but able-bodied men of say from 19-45, our army could not have numbered more than half a million. We had never prepared for war. And I am afraid to ask the question if you, Englishmen, were you ready in September 1939? Was any country, with the possible exception of Russia, adequately equipped to cross arms with our formidable neighbours?

Our activity lay in other directions. If a dry dock had to be taken from Portsmouth to Singapore there were captains of powerful tugs in Vlaardingen and Maassluis who liked to do the job; when a London-Melbourne race was organized we were among the first of the competitors. If you wanted choice fruit and fine cattle Holland could provide it—but tanks, heavy artillery, battleships, in a word a perfect machine for destruction of property and annihilation of human life—no, we had not.

Just before the war I attended a meeting of the borough-council of Margate where a scheme for the reorganization of elementary education happened to be put to the vote. It implied expenses over £100.000. In the preliminary discussions a teacher, one of the councilors, felt called upon to say a few words when one of the other men had hinted at the enormous amount of money involved and the raising of rates and taxes in consequence. "Let us not forget that we are in a country where we pride ourselves on distinguishing between tuition and education. If we want to act in accordance with this we must be prepared to pay for it. It is either 'cannon or butter' as some say, 'education or drill' as we prefer to put it."

Well, ninety-nine out of a hundred in our country would have backed this gentleman.

Some years before this meeting of the borough-council in Margate, a bill was proposed in our Second Chamber of Representatives which may be compared to your House of Commons, intended to grant the money for the construction of three battleships. You are a rich country, but you know that a modern battleship cannot be but a heavy tax on the financial budget of a small country. I have no memory for figures and so I forget how many millions of guilders the carrying of this plan would have cost. At the time we knew how many more teachers could be employed to reduce the number of pupils in our big classes; we knew how many schools could be built for the amount, how many students could be sent to Universities abroad to continue their studies as specialists in one field or another.

And we all went to Amsterdam where a hundred thousand voices were heard to protest against this expenditure of the money of an anti-militarist country.

And on the 10th of May we found ourselves opposed to a country that held the opposite views and had been working for years and years to prepare for the moment at which war—inevitable in their eyes—broke out.

Well, we did what we could. Fertile land was inundated, trenches were made, dug-outs appeared like mushrooms—our soldiers held them for a few days at the Grebbeberg—and our marines fought like devils on the bridges in Rotterdam. But our country was full of German maid-servants who had found employment with us, pretty full of German workmen and overseers in our factories, and we had our 4% of National Socialists who hailed their Aryan brethren from the other side of the Rhine as warriors in the same cause. It was not surprising that espionage became our strongest enemy. The city of Rotterdam was wiped out, we got an ultimatum that other towns, Utrecht among them, would follow if we did not capitulate.

Within a week this introduction to modern warfare had proved too much for us. Our queen, Princess Juliana, her husband and children, had been taken to England, and our Cabinet had followed and those who were left behind were extinguishing the flames in Rotterdam and burying the dead on the Grebbeberg.

The Time of Occupation: May 1940-June 1944

A Bird's Eye View

So we had lost our independence. Strange thought to have fought for it eighty years only to lose it again in 5 days. Dr. Seyss Inquart *(note: his official title was Reich Commissioner)*, who had done so much for the amalgamation of Austria in Das Gross-Deutsche Reich *(note: the Great German Reich)*, was on his way from Vienna. He was going to be our Governor. But we need not be afraid. "How could we, Germans, have acted otherwise?" they asked us. According to them they had plenty of evidence that the English intended to invade the Low Countries—"their 'Brittania rules the waves'" was going to simply add the coasts of Western Europe. The Rhine, not the North Sea, was meant to be England's frontier.

The Germans wanted to be looked upon as our protectors against this danger. Their government would not interfere with our interior political and economical interests. Although they had the right to show us the advantages of a National-Socialist State, the four percent of our population with their leader Mussert did their best to convince us that Utopia could not be far off. Some measures had to be taken, they were for our best. "You have lived as it were on an island far away from the turmoil of the world. In a land of dreams and idylls. You have not seen and you have not heard that a new world is being created – with equal opportunities for all, a world where 'labour' is enthroned and unemployment wiped out, where capitalism no longer exists and where a really great man—a gift from God—uses his talents and works day and night to bring about a wonderful transformation from chaos to order, from incurable disease to healthy, bubbling life."

The National-Socialist Movement donned their black shirts and waved their banners. Number one our programme: Trust in God, nr. 2 love of nation and country, nr. 3 respect of labour.

It must be said that the German soldier in general knew how to behave himself. I did not hear any complaint of those who had one or more of them quartered in their houses. Early in the morning they left without making unnecessary noise, in the evening they came in again wiping their feet or taking off their boots before going to bed. And they did not seem to appreciate the words of welcome or the German salutes from their Nazi brethren of Dutch blood.

But we were steadily going down the hill and the yoke put on with a light hand weighed upon us with ever increasing force. Did they keep their promise about not meddling with internal affairs. Did they try and put into practice this idea of equal opportunities for all men. Did they show that our fear of Prussianism was ill-founded?

Their propaganda for Arbeitsdienst—a term of Labour Service—did not seem so bad for those who from the very beginning were not prejudiced against everything that bore their name. Six months of manual labour, for young men of all classes in a camp, to teach them something of this—trust in God, love of nation and country, respect of labour. No insurmountable barriers between the sons of the manufacturer, the schoolmaster, the farm-hand. Need I tell you what points can be brought forward in support of such schemes? It can't be denied that there were a great many of us who lived by their brains or their pen who looked down on the man with the spade and the hammer. Something might be done to extirpate this.

"Mens sana in corpore sano." And now in good earnest, with the whole-hearted support of the Government itself. Why not?

But I saw something of this in a village where they were forming in hot haste the corps of officers who would have to train and educate these young men of eighteen. Those who had volunteered for such extension-courses after the compulsory 6 or 8 months necessarily came from the ranks of the National-Socialists. What I heard and saw was mere imitation of German soldiers' drill. Their words of command had been taken from the army, their shouting smacked of the Prussian 'Feldwebel' *(note: sergeant),* their shouldering and putting down of spades was dangerously alike the handling of a rifle.

You need not be surprised that those of us who were prepared to hold back unfavourable criticism until they had seen something of this "Arbeidsdienst" in practice soon gave it up as a bad job.

Another example.

We are not going to meddle with your internal politics. From May 1940 onward N.S.B. people were the only men who were appointed at government posts of any importance. As there were not enough capable men among their comparatively small number to fill them, many posts had to be entrusted to men who were absolutely unfit for them. Courses were being organized to form new burgomasters at short notice. A few months were considered to be sufficient for a barber, a farmer, a clerk to take the mayor's chair.

The results of their administration could not raise our expectations of Utopia as they saw it.

A nephew of mine applied for the post of attendant at the municipal museum at Utrecht. The first question put to him on presenting himself was: "Are you a member of the N.S.B.?" He had studied art for some years—as a matter of fact he had his certificate as a teacher of drawing. He had often led excursions to parts of our country, places of interest from a biological or historical point of view, but he was not a party man.

Second question: "If official guests of the city rang the bell or showed their cards would you be willing to salute them in New European fashion with the outstretched right arm?"

That was certainly asking too much of a young man who had once been a member of the A.J.C—an association of young men and women whose parents generally called themselves Social-Democrats.

One of the words embroidered in firm Gothic character on their German banners was: Kultur—culture with a capital. We have it on good authority that the Superintendent of our Royal Library at the Hague, the best collection of books in the whole country, was ordered to furnish the Governor's house with so many yards of voluminous and imposing-looking works—culture in concrete form in brown or red leather. One of the latest news bulletins speaks of a salt-mine in Germany where many pictures were found of old masters, among them many Rembrandts. A Committee will be formed to find out where these priceless objects of art came from.

Our periodicals dwindled to mere leaflets—bad paper, no illustrations; our papers completely lost their special character, our books were subjected to the censor, but the N.S.B organ was printed in extra-editions, and *Signaal,* a popular or if you prefer notorious magazine was published weekly—with the latest news from the front and the latest mass-executions by barbarians from both sides of the Ural mountains.

Our motor-cars gradually disappeared, so did our engines, our trucks, our carriages, our leather, our copper, our steel, our butter, our cheese, our potatoes, our fruit, our almost anything.

The German version was: in spite of the war we have seen to it that Holland's export has not fallen. If this can be achieved now, what inestimable profit it must be to Holland and to Rotterdam and Amsterdam in particular to have a Gross-Deutschland at their back with over 100 million, 200/300 million? inhabitants to consume their meat, to buy their eggs, to use their Fokker planes, to pile up their savings?

Here are some figures—in kilogrammes gross—for 1930 *(note: a kilogram is 2.2 lbs.)*. In 1940 they must have been higher. Fresh meat 36.000.000; margarine 72.000.000; butter 47.000.000; vegetables and fruit 547.000.000; sugar 102.000.000.

Margarine cannot be produced without raw material from Africa and India, but what about our meat, where is our fruit, our sugar, and why have the greengrocers struck work?

Education in general, the organization of our schools, in particular, is a subject to which I hope to give a special chapter.

But we must not conclude this survey of our sufferings in the four years of occupation before the invasion at Caen on the 6th of June 1944 without a few words of their attitude towards the Jews. It is true that there are many in our country—I know there are in yours—who do not look upon this part of the population with too friendly eyes. Is this sufficient to decide that they must be wiped out—enough reason to sterilize the men, to expel them from all public places, to drive them like cattle to concentration camps and torture them to death?

This in itself was sufficient for both our Protestant and Roman Catholic Churches to state that National-Socialism was incompatible with Christianity.

I hope that these few lines will show you that it was not all beer and skittles with us after we had laid down arms—that we had to pay the toll in this second great war. Our list of dead and maimed may not be so long as those of the Allies, but if all the executions, all the deaths through starvation, all the deranged minds, all the hardships count, we are not afraid to ask the question: What more could you have expected in the way of: be active where you can be useful and bear your sorrows in silence if they cannot be avoided?

The Schoolmaster Speaks

How was education affected during the years of occupation? What influence had the National-Socialist regime on the organization of our schools?

It was not long before all teachers had to sign a paper in which they declared that they would be loyal to the authorities of the occupation force and not do anything or take part in anything that was directed against them. For a civilian it was about the same thing as unconditional surrender for the soldier. The capitulation of our army was a fact— and we put our names at the bottom of the declaration. If you refused—I don't think there were many—It necessarily meant: discharge.

The beginning was only negative: you must not do this, stop that. But we had heard something of the development in Germany, in Austria, in Tsjecho-Slovakia. And we knew that the time could not be far off when they would go one step further. You must do this and you are expected to do that.

The influence on the curriculum was—for the secondary schools— fewer hours of English and French, more for German and the introductions of lessons in German at the elementary schools. There were not enough certificated men in those schools to give these lessons. But teachers of German could be stamped out of the ground like burgomasters. Were not there books on the market: English, French or German in 6 or even 3 months? It is true that the certificate of the lowest grade for a teacher of language was considered to take two years of continuous reading—but was not this rather long for a dynamic age of new powers?

All our text-books are subjected to the sharp eye of the censor. In our history book there was an illustration in the chapter on the Great War 1914-18. Underneath: The Big Four—Lloyd George, Clemenceau, Wilson and Orlando. It had to be cut out: Hindenburg and his staff were pasted in. In another book I used for translation purposes one of the fragments was on Churchill. No "Winston Churchill" in our schools. Louis Botha was considered better. I remember that in another book, Well-known, famous persons in history, Adolf Hitler was about the latest addition to the long list that began with Alexander the Great, perhaps before. The article was not in a vein of glorification and the book was put on the black list. Further use in school strictly prohibited. But we must not grumble too much at this. After all it is not pleasant to hear that the Führer of one's Heimatland is a man who on various occasions proved to be untrustworthy. But is not it silly to pronounce the verdict on a primer for reading in one of the lowest forms

of a school, because in one of the simple stories there is a boy called
Adolf who is kicked by a friend in a children's quarrel?

All references to our Queen and the living members of our Royal
house had to be suppressed. Even when the passage looked innocent
enough. Analyze this sentence: That day the Queen was too tired to
receive any guests.

> *Was too tired—predicate*
> *The guests—subject*

And so on. The word Queen must be made illegible—Insert
"mayor." But in the windows of the booksellers "Mein Kampf" was put
in a conspicuous place. Later on they tried to find buyers for a book for
children entitled: "Mother, tell me something more about Hitler,
please."

The books on history, natural as well as general, came off the worst.
The Batavians who from time immemorial had come floating down the
Rhine on trunks that had been hollowed to make a kind of primitive
canoe were no longer barbarians who hunted, gambled and made war,
leaving useful work to their wives. No, the ancestor of a German
National-Socialist of the 20th century had not received his due—no
gambling, no drinking, no barbarism.

Much stress had to be laid on the period when the Low Countries
formed part of the German Empire and it was a pity that the decline
during the Thirty Years' War had prevented them to see to it that we
could not carry off the victory in our Eighty Years' struggle for independence against the Spaniards.

But the worst thing in our schools is that we did not know what to
do with children of Dutch National-Socialists. The Dutch Scouts, naturally, had to disappear. Their hats were English, on their belts they had
the words: Be prepared and Lord Baden Powell was honoured as the
great founder of the organisation.

Instead of it all boys and girls in the Jeugdstorm, a pure emulation
of the Hitlerjugend and the Bund Deutsche Mädel. On Saturday after-
noons they held their meetings and in the morning the boys and girls
donned their uniforms and appeared at school in blue shirts, black and
orange caps.

If there was one part of our nation that could be called Anti-
National-Socialist, Anti-German, Anti-Mussert, etc. it was our
youth—the young men of 14-18, the girls under 20. Older people

might be skeptical, might dislike, disapprove. Our pupils were fanatical in their hatred, in their disgust of these classmates.

They made sneering remarks on their emblems, openly abused them, cut the tyres of their bikes, plagued them in all possible ways, until they perceived that their teachers, that the head was considered to be responsible for any signs of lack of discipline or disorder, fights in their schools.

It was not pleasant to see a popular teacher or the head who was not a bad sort arrested, sometimes sent to a camp, because one of the blue-shirts had got a black eye. In the end they changed their tactics and boycotted the Nazis.

What could the teachers do to wipe out this insurmountable barrier between boys and girls in the same class? Compromise was all but impossible. Do not forget that the percentage of pro's among teachers was even lower than that among the population as a whole.

At the time I was on the staffs of two schools. Among the thirty odd in the first there was one lady who was on the other side, in the second there was one man. One pro—30 anti.

We had always been taught no politics in council-schools. Now the precept was: open the minds of the boys, show them to the best of your ability the possibilities and advantages of National-Socialist Government.

The task was too much for some of us.

Dr. Gunning, the headmaster of my school in Amsterdam, was discharged. The letter in which he was informed of this decision of Mr. Seyss Inquart gave the following reasons: 1. You have allowed a class to be present at the graduation ceremony of a former Jewish teacher. 2. You have spoken words of eulogy for a Jew who founded sanatoriums or children's hospitals in your country.

When Jewish children were no longer allowed to attend our schools, some of the older pupils at a certain school were so enraged about this new measure that they wanted to compose a formal letter of protest to the burgomaster. Not knowing what was the best way to set about it they asked the advice of their teacher of geography. "Come to my house, and I'll help you." The letter was sent, the way in which it had been written found out, the teacher was discharged.

The head of my second school was carried off as hostage to a camp where he had to stay for nine months. Later on the National-Socialists frankly declared that it was his own doing—the Head ought to have seen to it that the man's daughter could go to school without being molested or hindered in any way by her class mates.

What four years of German protection did at the two schools where I worked?

The headmaster of one school discharged, of the other, lifted from his bed and take to a camp as hostage. He had a nervous breakdown after he had returned and resumed his regular work.

One of the colleagues was accused of helping Jews—taken to prison—his wife was informed of his death 8 or ten days after the event. It was given out that he had sprung down from a balcony and taken his own life. Our new headmaster who knew him well said: "A. committing suicide? Impossible."

Another had his house searched. Distribution cards were found scattered on a table. Evidently intercepted before they could be sent to people who could not provide themselves with these valuable papers in the ordinary way. He and his wife were transported to Vught, and Vught at one time was looked upon as the worst concentration camp in Holland. Up to now we do not know what has happened to him.

Two colleagues at one of the schools, one lady at the other were Jews. We do not know where or how they died or whether they are still alive.

A teacher of mathematics could not control himself when Jews in or near his house were roughhandled. He was arrested, afterwards discharged.

In one of the *razzias* another had the ill-fortune to see his way of escape blocked. His group was sent to Arnhem. Before they got so far, he committed suicide. We do not know the exact circumstances.

One of our best men—his heart in his work and perhaps as representative for the school as the head himself—died a few months ago. Was it really cancer or starvation?

We do not know.

Is this list long enough? Did we pay our toll in this total war, although none of them were killed in a bombardment, although none of them wore khaki?

On the Eve of the Landing—at Caen

In our bird's eye view of the period 1940-1944 we did not say much about the war as it was carried on in and out of Europe. And we need not spend much time on it as you know the facts as well or better than we do.

At the beginning the German Blitzkrieg with the motorized troops swiftly advanced in Holland, in Flanders, to Paris, to the coast of France. In the East less quickly and not as it were in one breath they pushed forward to Moscow and Stalingrad. In the extreme South they planted their Hakenkreuz *(note: swastika)* on the tops of the Caucasus. They crossed the Mediterranean and were not so very far from Alexandria and Cairo.

The Organisation Todt *(note: created in 1938, a vast forced labor bureaucracy)* built an Atlantic wall from Bayonne on the Spanish frontier to Hammerfest and the reindeer in the North. At one time it seemed as if the whole of Europe was going to be under German control. Switzerland, Spain and Sweden were the only countries which had been able to maintain a state of neutrality. Neutrality, by the way, was impossible in German eyes. It was either pro or anti—with us or against us.

Then came the moment of counter-attacks, the Russians first, the English and Americans later on. The slow but steady retreat from Stalingrad, the campaign in Africa, Lampedura, Panetellaria. Nelluno was important, the capture of Mussolini seemed so, but it was not. The Nazis made a second-rate thriller or an American film of the bad sort out of his liberation by S.S. troops.

The worst blow to them must have been the early date at which America decided to join the Allies.

Some time ago I saw a book on American Government in a second-hand bookshop. One chapter for each of their departments. This is what I found in the chapter on the War Department. The figures may give you some idea of the gigantic possibilities of the U.S., a quarter of a century ago.

"There were those who argued that manpower would defeat Germany. The U.S. mobilized 5,000,000 men to go to France, or half as many as the total number of soldiers then in the struggle. Behind the first 5,000,000 the nation prepared to call out another equal number if necessary. It required the arrival in France of only 2,000,000 of the first 5,000,000 to make Germany sue for peace. Hindenburg, the great German commander, in his postwar book, admits that Germany did not believe United States could accomplish such a result. The German General Staff learned the actual size of the American Expeditionary Forces only when it struck the German lines like a tidal wave.

There were those who argued that sufficient artillery would destroy Germany. The Army had in full swing when the war ended a gun production program that would have supported and supplied all the allied forces, as well as the American Army, with all the guns of every size they could use. The largest guns actually used in the war were 16-inch weapons which hurled shells weighing over a ton more than 15 miles. The army was equipped, at the close of the war, to turn out 20-inch guns with a range of 25 miles and to throw shells a ton and a half.

There are those who believed that aircraft would win the war. The Army took over the job of building them. The first step was the production of the Liberty motor, the most powerful aircraft engine turned out during the war. The next was to learn how to build airplanes. Before the war ended the fore-runners of the American-built air fleet that would have certainly numbered tens of thousands of planes had arrived in France. At home the country was full of Liberty motors, so full that thousands could be spared for France, England and Italy to use.

There were those who believed tanks would win the war. The Army undertook, in cooperation with the British, to turn out enough of these land battleships for both the American and British Armies. They were to range from the little two-men "whippets" to the great 40-ton "Mark VIIIs" with twelve men and half a dozen guns aboard. The caterpillar traction idea that made tanks a possible weapon was an American idea. In the joint program, America fabricated part of the tanks and shipped them to England for completion and issue. Then, on its reserve resources, America started a separate tank program of its own, greater than the whole joint effort. The Army has two score of the 40-tonners to-day as a result of that program.

There were those who argued that gas would win the war. The Army began the manufacture of gas on a scale no other country, not even Germany, could possibly attain. It mobilized scientific brains to produce new and more deadly gases. The war ended with the gas program just getting into full swing. Since the war, the U.S. with other powers has resolved against the use of poison gases as inhuman because the injury they do cannot be confined to the fighting forces. Civilian populations, without means of protection, are apt to be engulfed in wind-driven gas clouds intended for the troops. The American Army is to-day equipped to protect itself from gas attack, but would employ gas itself only after it had been attacked.

If they could do this in 1917, what might not they do in this war? The man who made farmers' tools, must turn his hand to rifles and machine-guns, the man who turned out planes for commercial purposes must be set to work on modern bombers and chasers, the man in the shipbuilding yard would have to put submarines, destroyers, battleships and aircraft carriers on the stocks and Ford would have to supply armoured cars and tanks.

But if they had all started on this new work what country in the world could be successful in opposing them?"

What we saw of all this in our own country?

Barbed wire was fixed everywhere, tank-moats were dug, new flying grounds were laid out, beautiful woods had to disappear, and dunes were made into one long series of dug-outs, parts of fertile country were inundated, fruit trees in the orchards cut down. And in the streets we heard the rhythmic beat of the hob-nailed boots of the German soldiers to the tune of "Wir fahren nach England."

And they did make services preparations. Our ships were gone, but our river barges were coupled side by side and a powerful tug would do the rest. As soon as they had put out to sea, British reconnoitering planes and patrolling destroyers sent them to the bottom of the North Sea. The plan was abandoned. They kept up their song "Wir fahren" for a while, it dwindled and finally it was given up.

The bombardments of the Allies of our towns were a heavy tax on our friendly feelings towards them. But while we were burying our dead at Nieuwegein, at Enschede, at the Hague, and looking after our wounded, we tried to see it in the light of military necessity, our share in the greatest ordeal the world has ever seen.

Food rations were steadily going down. Diphtheria, typhoid fever every week brought hundreds of new victims. All medicines to fight dysentery were gone. There was no wood to make coffins for the dead, no morphine to relieve the pain of the suffering, no bandages to dress the wounds, no restoratives for those who had the good fortune to find the way to recovery.

You need not be surprised that the 6th of June 1944 was looked upon as a momentous day in our country.

When they came back
21 Apr. 1945
The dikes at Muiden have been pierced, the Meent at Huizen and Eemnes is inundated. So is the Wieringermeer. Grim fighting neat Putten, Harderwijk. Mr. van Beusekom told the boys to go home and wait for the letter informing them of resumption of lessons at school.

It is difficult to go on with my story. For today is the 21th of April 1945 and the Allies are reported to have pushed forward to about one or two miles from Amersfoort. And Amersfoort is only one hour on one's bike from the place where I am writing. They may be here tomorrow and it may take another week. What are the Germans going to do, defend themselves to the bitter end or raise the white flag as soon as the first Canadian tanks come in sight? It seems pure luck whether a town or village comes off unscathed or is raised to the ground. Zutphen and Deventer are said to be all but wiped out, Groningen is not so bad and Leeuwarden is practically untouched.

But it must be done: did I not call my report The Great Second War—Looking Backward?

So I open my map world atlas of "Everyman's Encyclopaedia" and turn to page 75: Northern France. And my thoughts go back to the sixth of June. English and Americans took the step for which we had been waiting so long. They had landed near Caen. And the Atlantic Wall had been unable to hold them. The news-bulletins of our illegal parties were very optimistic. Now or never. Was this the moment for which Herr Hitler had been waiting so long? Had not we heard on various occasions that the Führer would be only too glad to come to blows with the Anglo-Americans once more? Had not he bragged: let them ask me a place where they would like to land their troops. I am prepared to withdraw my German divisions from the spot until they have comfortably transported men and arms. And then, one more battle, a decisive battle this time. I am not at all in doubt about the ultimate winner.

The first report we had indicated that the introductory phase of this military exploit was different. As it always was in this war. Nine predictions out of ten never came true.

The Germans fought like devils and did their best to prevent a comeback of their enemies from the very beginning. And according to our papers the prospects of the Allies were far from encouraging. As luck would have it, the day fixed for the big venture brought a rough sea. And the poor English soldiers got seasick in the Channel and were not in the best of conditions when they heard the command: Forward my men, straight on, right to the Siegfried line. The heavy artillery first, the machine guns later on, played havoc among them and according to Mr. Blokzijl, the leader of our Nazi press, the beach at Caen was covered with dead and wounded scattered among the burning remains of boats, tanks and other arms.

Progress was slow and wearisome indeed, and far too slow for us. For we were always impatient and far more so as circumstances became worse. But after a few weeks, it was a pleasure to take up the map once more; every new day other places were mentioned. Those were the days of Caen, Tilly, Bayeux, Carentan, Argentan, Rennes, etc. We heard about Cherbourg, of the Americans on their way to Brest, and after the collapse of the German front of Lisieux, Evreux, Mantes, Paris.

The attempt to reestablish the two fronts had succeeded. Englishmen, Canadians and Americans fighting in the West, Russians in the East.

How we were informed about things as they were? As you know, a long time before the Germans had compelled us to deliver our wireless sets. But some of them only moved from a conspicuous place in the front room to a snug corner in another apartment.

So we knew what the B.B.C. said to you—we had our own broadcast in Dutch from London, the illegal parties issued their bulletins every day, later on thrice a week, and Hilversum gave the German version. If you were wise you took the news from both sides and 20 English miles + 10 German miles divided by 2 made 15, the number that was probably not far wrong.

When the Germans were steadily driven back, after Brussels and Antwerp had fallen, our Government in London ordered the railways to go on strike and it was promptly followed up. If ever there was an example of unanimous, undivided resistance it was the attitude of the thousands of men employed by the Dutch Railways.

Their wages were stopped of course, but already in the first few weeks the money given to support them was calculated to cover a period of so many months.

What was the ultimate effect of this strike on the Dutch people as a whole? It soon became evident that this unforeseen course of events was a very sore point with our protectors. All the other means of transport were requisitioned immediately. The motor cars that had been left to us disappeared and very soon our bikes, too, were taken away from us.

You are not a cycling nation. So you cannot imagine what a blow it is for a Dutchman. An American without a car is bad, an Englishman without a cricket bat is worse, but a Dutchman without a bike is undoubtedly the worst.

Let me tell you what it meant to us at the time of the war in the next chapter which will bear the short title: Food.

Food

With five years of occupation it is difficult not to be influenced by the ruling authorities. There is first of all their language. If ever our language was threatened by German contamination, it is how we used to speak about Leger. "Wehrmacht" is much more familiar to us now. A man who has succeeded in obtaining a document stating that he is exempted from work abroad—read "Germany"—shows his "Ausweis," the word Vrijstelling has gone out of use. It takes some thinking to realize that "Ortscommandant" stands for Plaatselijke bevelhebber, that Sperrgebied simply means "Verboden terrein."

And so on.

Must it be looked upon as another instance of German influence that I spent some hours this Sunday morning perusing the Annual Pocketbooks of the Central Bureau of Statistics? The love of statistics and their inexhaustible thirst for figures is well known is it not? But in this case the influence need not be contagious in a bad sense. If I must write something about our food position in 1944 and '45, it may be instructive to begin with a few figures that may give the reader an idea of the possibilities of our country in the way of agricultural products and dairy products before the war. I borrowed my data from the yearbooks for 1940, 1941 and 1942. It is interesting to see that some of the usual chapters contain new figures for the last year.

Our population
for 1939   8.883.977
for 1940   8.923.245
for 1941   9.007.722

For reasons that are not difficult to guess the later volumes do not give any new information about agriculture, cattle breeding, horticulture, commerce, etc.

If the present rations can be explained in some or any way, it does not seem unreasonable to quote some figures from Chapter VII "Industry and Trade" of the above mentioned publication for 1942.

What our farmers did in 1939			What they had in stables, meadows
	h.a.(hectare)	1000kg.	2.817.314 cows
wheat	123.864	416.528	(is that not 1 cow for every 3 persons?)
Rye	225.345	603.532	689.501 sheep
Pulse	60.198	185.891	1.553.413 pigs
potatoes	95.838	2.231.520	32.804.504 chickens that worked all the
meat		398.209	year to produce 146.928.000 kg. eggs.
milk		1.082.860	
butter		108.533	
cheese		120.828	
condensed milk		143.021	

I took the trouble to see how this worked out per head and per day. Our home produce would have been sufficient to give us every day of the year 310 gr. Bread, 2/3 kg. potatoes, 50 gr, peas and beans, 100 gr. meat (beef and pork), 1/3 l. milk, 33 gr. butter, nearly $\frac{1}{2}$ pound a week, cheese 36 gr.—half a pound a week, condensed milk 44 gr.—3 ounces a week *(note: l. is liter)*.

And now the railways strike.

Even in 1944 the Germans said it would be possible to provide the Dutch people with sufficient food. Why should they dig their own graves by depriving themselves of the means of transport to convey the food from the areas of production to the consumers? What the Government, what the emigrants in London achieved with their idiotic, shortsighted command was starvation of their fellow-countrymen, while the object, obstruction of all conveyance of German troops and war material was not hampered at all. They had the rolling stock and sufficient railway employees of German blood to run the trains necessary for their own private use.

Although they had done their best to make us acquainted with their system of transfusing knowledge, their way of imbuing us with culture, we had enough brains left to ask the questions:

Was it the custom to convey potatoes and corn from the country to town by means of the railway? If they had enough rolling stock and men for their own private purposes, was it necessary to take our cars, our trucks, even our bicycles?

In 1939 3.700.000 Dutchmen paid f. 3 to get the little label which they had to fix to their machines in order to avoid difficulties with the police. 3.700.000 bikes and 8.883.977 people. If one does not count the babies and young children to five or six, the older people who preferred the pavement and a stick, it is remarkable that there were any Dutchmen who walked left. No tax, no rate was more unpopular than the annual f. 3 for the bike *(note: f. is Dutch guilder, approximately $0.45 in 1940)*.

And these bicycles had to be surrendered. Hand them in to the German authorities, and you will get a paper bearing the Imperial Eagle entitling the holder to so many marks and guilders to be paid after the war. In this case it was not so easy and not so efficient to say "No!" as with the wireless set. What is the value of a means of conveyance if it is taken to pieces or buried? Those who risked it were in constant danger of being accosted by a German soldier: *"Ausweis bitte."* Later on without the *"bitte."*

By the time they thought it necessary to requisition our bicycles for the Wehrmacht these parts of our outdoor equipment had become even more indispensable than in normal times. The pre-war models with air-filled tubes, those with solid tyres, the newer sort provided with wooden tyres and the latest invention without any tyres, they were all used for foraging purposes. When the government could no longer distribute the necessary food, every Dutchman was left to his own resources to make good the ever growing deficiency. The next chapter will give you an idea of what kind these bicycle tours were and are.

And how indispensable to keep body and soul together. Here is the latest news as regards provisions for the week 23 Apr.-28 Apr.

1945: 400 gr. of bread, 1kg. of potatoes for those who do not get their food from the Central Kitchen.

Can one live on 60 gr. of bread and 140 gr. of potatoes a day?

But the central kitchen? This week the menu was: 6 times soup, half a liter of water + something that is difficult to analyze, once mashed potatoes with cabbages, ½l.

When the Government Fails: Foraging
One Sunday afternoon, the beginning of February 1945

My first journey in search of the necessary food was made between Christmas and New Year. After some weeks the potatoes I had been able to bring home were rapidly decreasing, but it was so bitterly cold and the snowfall making another trip in the same way with a three-wheeled bicycle absolutely impossible, I had to put off my second journey from day to day.

But on this memorable Sunday the thermometer was still several degrees below zero. I said to my wife: "Why put our heads in the sand like so many ostriches any longer? Tell me how many days can you manage." She made a thorough investigation of all that could be considered eatable and then gave out the ultimatum: four days! Monday the weather could not have been worse. Snow storms, hail now and then, a pretty strong wind blowing from the South-West. Starting that day would inevitably have meant defeat by the elements, and with my constitution at that time almost certainly a cold, the flu or worse. We decided to wait another day. Tuesday morning. Still snowing. But we could not wait for ever. At half past ten I said: "I'm off." With my leather coat, ear warmers, clogs, two pair of socks, I did go.

The first 15 miles or so to Amsterdam I had the wind blowing sideways, right across the road. I was covered with frozen snow and ice. It was all I could do to keep to the middle. At the sides slipping away was a dead certainty. After some nasty falls and a couple of hours stiff wind I reached Amsterdam.

I shall never forget the dreary atmosphere hanging over this town. You do not know the Amsterdammer, but he is one of the best sort of town-bred people to be found in our country. Always ready with his jokes, frank, hospitable and certainly the last to be down-hearted. The people, and there were not many in the thoroughfares, passed each other in silence. I did not hear one man speaking to another for miles through the centre of this once lively seaport town. The snow was not shoveled away. I passed a hearse, a farmer's horse in front., one single man in black with drooping shoulders and bent head at the back. It was a time that coffins were no longer available. So this was probably a man, or a woman borne to the cemetery in a cardboard box or simply sewn up in a sheet.

The shops were closed, in the restaurants, the hotels no sign of life. My way led through the Jewish quarters. All the houses empty, everywhere broken windows. At frequent intervals open spaces with heaps of stones, charred wood, old bottles, broken down furniture.

At the ferry across the Ij of the six boats in normal times only one in operation. At the other side the long struggle against snowdrifts, slippery ice and a bleak wind was continued.

Five o'clock Purmerend. It might be possible to go on to Hoorn before dark and Hoorn was only eight miles from my destination. As the only hotelkeeper I knew in the place had no room for me that night, there was no other possibility. Tired and rather cold I went on again. A dull, grey sky brought twilight and complete darkness before I reached the next town. Just before it a high dyke of about 2 miles. Along the Yselmeer Lakes on to the old market town. I could not see my way, only feel it. Snow up to the knees meant too far to the right, a steep slope with a frozen ditch at the bottom. 10 yards further down too far to the left. Let it suffice to say I was not cold anymore when, all but exhausted, I saw the dim outlines of houses in front.

That was 10 miles from Venhuizen, the little village at the end of my journey. Ten miles from my destination and friends. But I felt like a beggar when I had to look for a place to rest in the dark of an unknown town. No hotel, no restaurant showing signs of life at my knocking.

With the help of a woman who had paid a visit to a neighbour and was just going home, I found the orphanage. They took me in, gave me a bed with three blankets and I lay down with an inferiority complex— well developed. During the night the thermometer suddenly rose and I heard water dripping from the gutter. The road had completely changed, mud instead of ice, rain instead of hail.

It was impossible to cycle. Never mind, a walk of 8 or 10 miles with the sun peeping through the clouds would not kill me. At about 2 o'clock I was at Venhuizen, where my friends of the May days 1940 lived. A former visit had taught me that they could not do anything for me. When the unending, daily stream from Amsterdam had come upon them, they had helped when and where they could.

After this there had been a period of selling, first at reasonable prices, later on at exorbitant prices. Now, February 1945 not a kg. of potatoes, not a pound of beans or peas, could be had for love of money. It was all exchanging.

One need not believe all the stories to show what a complex revolution in the relative value of various goods a few months of ever growing want had brought about. What I heard and saw with my own eyes may be sufficient. In the week that I came a man had knocked on the door of the mother of one of the ladies I happened to know.

"Have you got any potatoes for me, please?" "Sorry, man, we have not." "But I am willing to give you my wedding ring for them." "If I could, I would. The potatoes we have are barely sufficient for our own private use. Just for curiosity's sake, what do you expect to get for that ring?" "Well, madam, I should be only too glad to get 25 kg. for it." A little arithmetic will show you that with our cooked meals twice a day— the bread rations had fallen to 600 gr. a week—this plain old ring would have been sufficient for a family of father, mother and two children for one week.

At the house of a well-to-do-farmer a boy did his best to get something: "What have you got to change?" "Nothing, only money." " I don't want your money. You know as well as I do, money is of no use whatever. But what about the shoes you are wearing." "Do you mean that." "Of course, no shoes for me, no potatoes for you." The boy from Amsterdam took them off, went back with a 'half mud', ±35 kg. of potatoes, barefooted. A policeman addressed him, enquired into the matter and the farmer was told to return the shoes after he had the impudence to ask for his potatoes.

My personal experience was:

20 pounds of peas for a boy's overcoat in good condition and four weeks later when the market had risen again: 25kg of potatoes and 25 kg. of carrots for a piece of flannel enough for 2 pairs of children's pyjamas, a woolen pull-over practically new and 2 blankets for a baby's cradle.

I was present when another transaction took place: three shirts, three pair of pants and a lady's dressing gown, all of excellent pre-war quality and brand new for 25 kg. of potatoes.

This story would not be complete and unfair to the farmers if we did not mention the deplorable experiences many of them had with people they had kindly taken in when the falling evening or 8 o'clock, the time for getting indoors, had overtaken them.

In the morning the hosts missed their sheets, or other valuable articles and when the guests were removed to the stable or to the barn, they found one or more of their chickens gone in the morning after the visitors had left.

I was not surprised to find notices at the gates of some of the farms: "People from Amsterdam are not allowed to enter."

On the way back the wind was dead against me and I had to walk more than half of the 50 miles, but when after four days of hard work I came home again, we could expect to keep the enemy "hunger" from our doors for another few weeks.

25 Apr. 1945.

My wife bought 2 pounds of wheat for f. 50. Tulip bulbs do not agree with me and we must have something for breakfast.

Vegetables are sold in the morning, rhubarb, spinach and leek—prices sky-high. Those who cannot afford to pay what they ask may come back in the afternoon at half past two, form a queue and wait until they hear the man say: sorry, sold out. In the afternoon, it's going to be salad—25 c. a head.

Razzia

Foraging was largely a story of my own experiences. So is this chapter. At the end of 1944 the word "razzia" was not unknown to us for it was the German way, especially in Amsterdam, to hunt down Jews who had preferred keeping in hiding to answering the summons of their oppressors to await their further orders. If they were allowed to go home again provided with a yellow star on the breast of their coats they were lucky. But later on the harbingers of the new era made a clean sweep of everything that was not Aryan. Whole districts were surrounded by a close ring of soldiers; others were ordered to search the houses thoroughly. They must have achieved their purpose for the last year or so we have not seen a single Jew with or without the offensive emblem. "Today it is us, tomorrow you." This tomorrow came for us in the autumn of 1944. One morning we were awakened by the unpleasant sound that had only been used at regular intervals for tests to see if they were operating well and our local papers had always informed us beforehand when this was going to take place. Besides we did not hear the engines of any aircraft. We had heard of razzias in Hilversum the day before and Hilversum is only four miles from our own place, but at the end of the fourth year many of us were so fed up with the countless rumours which afterwards appeared to have had no foundation whatever, that we did not easily believe things until we saw them with our own eyes or heard with our own ears.

But we jumped out of bed and ran to the window. Two sons and a friend of my neighbour were already in the garden in pyjamas or half-dressed trying to make their escape. They beckoned to me to follow their example. Even then I remained rather calm and decided to stay indoors. I asked my wife to go to the head of the school who did not live far off to ask if he intended to continue lessons at school or not. She was back again after five minutes and told me that Mr. H. was no longer at home. He had fled and his wife advised me to do the same. If I knocked at a certain door, mentioned his name I would no doubt be admitted and find a hiding place that was considered to be safe.

As my wife had seen sentries in one or two places it could no longer be doubted that the danger of being taken away was very great indeed. At the moment that I left the house on my bike, my wife on the carrier to have a look around the corners before I followed, there was a soldier at the end of our street about 60 yards away and another had been posted round the corner—we had to pass him at a distance of 40 yards.

There was not much time to decide: return and be caught at home or go on and take the risk of being shot or blown up by a hand grenade. We could see that they had been amply provided with them. The man was whistling a tune, not *"Wir fahren nach England,"* did not stop when we passed him and we knew that a nasty cliff had been rounded. I knocked at the door that had been indicated to me, mentioned the name of the Head and a few moments later I was between two solid concrete floors about one yard from each other in the company of about ten other men who had arrived before me and were congratulating one another that the first attempt to catch them had failed. But we felt only comparatively safe. At the time we did not know that our place of refuge was not to be trespassed upon even by the German soldiers without special permits. It was pitch dark and all sound from outside could only reach us in a transformed, unfamiliar way. Mr Seyss Inquart could not say any longer that we, in Holland, were living in an idyll.

The first news that penetrated from outside was: the Germans are now in the streets with cars provided with loudspeakers. Every man between 18 and 50 must go to the municipal park; he will have to work, but there are good wages for him at the end of the week and plenty of food three times a day. Those who do not act in accordance with this proclamation and are found in hiding shall be shot on the spot. Another decision had to be taken. We all remained where we were. Later in the evening the prisoners were aired and got some warm food at the house of one of them, but the information as to the sentries having been withdrawn or still at their posts being contradictory we went down into the cellar again where we spent the night.

The following morning we breakfasted on what we had brought down the evening before and were told by those who kept contact with the outer world for us that two men who had tried to escape the day before had been shot. One head attempted to flee from the roof. When he did not answer the command of a German boy in the street to come down, three shots—one through the heart—had killed him. A good shot, this young man. Mr. Baldur von Schirach *(note: German Youth Leader)* had shown once more that the proper handling of a rifle could not be taught too early.

In the course of that day peace seemed to have returned in the village and we went our several ways to go home. I had not gone very far when I was warned that in the street where I lived they had just returned to search again. Afterwards I heard that they had been there a second time but early in the morning. I slept between the tiles and some panelling in the attic that night.

But the next day, we all were in our own beds again. 1500-2000 men were not. They had been transported to Arnhem and had to dig trenches, make barricades to keep our Allies out of the Northern provinces.

30 Nov. 1944

It was not long after these days of razzia in Bussum and Naarden that I went out one morning to go to the house of a friend of mine, a teacher of manual labour. Santa Claus drawing near, I intended to make a book rack for my son. My friend had a bench and the necessary tools—a few hours every day in his workshop and I might be able to surprise Peter on the 5th of December. When I was busy with chisel and hammer, I heard the yapping rat-tat of aircraft guns. As we had got quite accustomed to the visits of patrolling chasers which evidently had been ordered to make all traffic on road and railway impossible, I did not pay much attention to it. After a short interval the machine guns played again. This time the grim rattle was broken by louder reports as if light bombs had been dropped. A train had passed a few minutes before and this must have been their target. Even then I did not find it worth my while to stop working. I took my hammer again and intended to go on for another half hour. My friend's son, however, had taken his bike to find out what had happened. His way led him past our house where my wife had told him that I better come home. I knew she was easily upset, so I took off my overalls and went. At the level crossing I found the train which I had heard some time before. Probably the boiler of the engine riddled with bullets, but the first goods vans behind were in flames.

Loud reports at regular intervals showed that they had been loaded with ammunition and one case after another was blown up. At the corner of the next street I found wife, son and mother-in-law with hand luggage in a state of great agitation.

The police had ordered them to leave the house as a train with explosives had been hit and they did not know what was going to happen with the houses along or near the railway. We lived a distance of about a hundred yards from the line.

We put down our things at the house of an acquaintance and could not do anything but wait. Later in the afternoon of that day the people who lived in our quarter were allowed to return to the houses and see what they could do. We soon saw that we might not find things in the same state in which we had left them. And our house proved to be one of the worst. In front and at the side all the windows were smashed. The ceiling of the study of the first floor had partly come down, the partition wall between it and the bedroom behind had disappeared. My big book case had toppled over and a heavy wash stand had been dropped upon it. It was quite clear that it would be impossible to make it habitable again. So all our energy was at once directed towards moving to another place and that as quickly as possible.

The weather might change and if it began to rain, what with the
leaking roof and the state of the ceiling between the floors, our furniture or what was left of it might be spoilt.

A colleague had said to the authorities when they were collecting
names of people who had plenty of room that he was willing to take 2
or 3 evacuated persons if necessary. He had had three of them for a couple of weeks. When I told him my story he said that his guests had just
left. They had found that a relation of theirs whom they had lost sight
of had lived at Bussum and they had moved to their family. If I would
have a look at the apartment they had used. In practice it would come
to this: a large living room and closed verandah that could be turned
into a bedroom for ourselves, his study for himself and me, the kitchen
for both of us. I was as pleased as Punch and said: "Of course."

It was not easy to find a man who could move our furniture. A *pan-
technicon (note: furniture van)* with 3 men from Amsterdam worked for us
from half past one till half past four. "What shall I put you down for,
Sir?" the boss said at the end when I had worked at least as hard as they.
"I don't know, my man, it is your daily work." "Well, let us say f. 130
then, everything included." For f. 130 one could have 3 men for that
kind of work a whole week instead of three hours. Have not you got the
English proverb: One man's death is another man's breath?

But we were glad that after eight or ten days we could sleep in our
own beds again and that our own table, chairs and the rest had found a
good place in new surroundings.

The Winter 1944-'45

It was not pleasant, the last winter of the war in Holland. It is the
last, is not it? Today, the 28th of April, the bridges of the fortress of
Naarden have been blown up, all but one. The German soldiers have
made many of our roads impassable, the polders around us are inundated, but the Italians are said to have risen in revolt, Mussolini has fled.
General Dittmar, the press-correspondent for the German army has
been captured, Göring has retired *(note: Head of Luftwaffe, at one point
designated as Hitler's successor).*

It is said that a weak heart has forced him to take this step. I
should not wonder, if his heart had something to complain of, for the
field marshall *was* rather fat, was not he? The Russians have penetrated

into Berlin, and all action at the front in our country has been suspended because a breakdown in Germany can't be far off.

Well, it was a winter without coal, without gas, later on without electricity and the last few weeks the water supply has been practically cut off.

No coal meant cutting trees and dragging wood, sawing and chopping one hour every day: no electricity meant going to bed at eight o'clock or spoiling your eyes with a candle or a diminutive oil-wick; no water going to a pump in the neighbourhood to get in buckets what we used in barrels before. Distribution gradually got less practical value; at present our rations have fallen to 400 gr. of bread, 1 kg. of potatoes, the children have been promised 12 l. of milk for the next month, but the milkman only shrugs his shoulders and says: "Tell me where to get it."

But the old habit of sending each other Christmas greetings was kept up. A friend of mine who has a poetic vein sent it in these words:

> Our days are born in pain and die in sorrow,
> And thread themselves to one long string of grief;
> Our stores are dwindling fast. Where can we borrow
> A thought of hope and cheer, forever brief?
>
> Our rooms are chill, our empty stomachs praying,
> Care chiselled lines where kindly smiles have fled;
> The homeless through the countryside are straying;
> Shrill sirens shrieks where mirth and song are dead.
>
> Rains stripes the even days, and seem unending,
> Vast gleaming wastes our fertile fields submerge;
> The trees are drooping, their bare branches sending
> A song of mourning down, a dripping dirge.
>
> Our days are born in pain and die in sorrow,
> The willing twigs are dripping their sad dirge.....
> But in the stem life struggles with to-morrow,
> And, conquering, in beauty will emerge!
>
> The sun above the grey his day is biding
> To set the earth and all the sky aglow;
> Through grief the world to happiness is gliding....
> The snowdrop blows beneath a layer of snow.

Once in the darkness wondrous bells were pealing;
Through twenty centuries we hear their call;
A child said: "Fear not, though thy world is reeling."
Who loses hope and faith, he loses all!

Dec. 10th 1944
Mr. and Mrs. v.d. Keuken-Heymel
wishing their friends and relations
A Happy New Year

At school we made desperate attempts to keep things going. When it became too cold to have them in our temporary residence the whole day, lessons were reduced to two hours a day either late in the morning or early in the afternoon, as we had to share the building with another school that had been driven out. When this was no longer possible we asked the parents to come to our assistance. Could they receive us in little groups, Mr. A. this week, Mrs. B. the next? We did this for another few weeks. Then the Germans intervened again, because the 8th of January 1945 it was impossible for all men under forty to go out.

Some weeks after this they did not observe this limit any more and men up to seventy had to dig or were commandeered for fatigue duty. We did not give up yet. We tried to do something with tasks to be given one week, to be handed in the next. And then—it was in the middle of April the head announced that lessons would be suspended until peace had been concluded.

This brings my tale up-to-date, and the rest of the story if it be written at all will have another character, more like a diary.

Must we sum up and say some word in conclusion to show what effect all this had on our people in general, on myself? Did these years of war prove what our Nazi-friends tried to make us believe? In war the best qualities in a man are awakened, it furthers Kameradschaft, i.e. friendliness, Treue, i.e. loyalty, Ehre—honour. Many untruths have been passed on us, the grossest lies were deliberately used for propaganda purposes, but this glorification of fröhliche Krieg—Merry War, was certainly one of the worst.

What I saw and what I heard leads me to say:

If ever there was a time in which civilization was shown in its true, unvarnished colours it is now. Those of us who had no sterling values were exposed without reserve, there was little hospitality, little broad-mindedness, little friendliness, little Christian feeling, much shortsightedness, vulgarity and egotism.

But we read "Hamlet" on Wednesday evenings with a little group of seven this winter. We never liked the teacher's job so much as in these days and the intention to work for a better world is very strong in most of us.

A world with less blood, less cruelty, less egotism, more flowers in untainted air under brighter skies.

28 April 1945

Radishes 35 c a bunch, cauliflower f. 3.50 as large as a man's fist f. 4.50 slightly bigger than that.
Bought 2 pounds of meat for f. 64, one pound of salt for f. 15
Rumours of armistice. No booming of heavy artillery, no machine
Guns of diving aircraft the last two days.
Next week 8th packet of the Swedish Red Cross.
I am reading: "Grapes of Wrath" by Steinbeck.

> Even in peace all is not beer and skittles
> Yet, give us peace, oh Lord—

From day to day

30 April 1945

Is Mussolini dead? And Göring? Where is Hitler?
Himmler talking about capitulation with the Allies?
Yesterday, packets with food were dropped near Rotterdam, The Hague and Leyden. The plan was to drop red and green torches to indicate the spot where the valuable contents were to follow. 600 tons to make a beginning. Not too bad.

The official prices for vegetables as published on a board at the police-station are as follows:

salad per head	50 c.
endive per kg	450 c.
salad for cooking	200 c.
spinach	300 c.
radishes per bunch	60 c.
carrots	400 c.

Calling on a colleague yesterday they told us that they had bought half a cheese, 6 pounds, à f. 40 a pound. It was rather more than what they intended to buy. We could have part of it. Went home with 1 pound 320 gr. Price f. 65.60.

2 May 1945

No capitulation yet. But—the Allies & the Germans have come to an agreement to prevent starvation of the Dutch still living in occupied districts. A committee of five have been appointed to work out plans immediately: One American, an Englishman, a German, Prince Bernhard, Seyss Inquart.

And how promptly they executed these plans. This morning we saw the bombers right over our heads. Crailoo was one of the spots where the food had to be dropped. Did not we wave our handkerchiefs like mad!

Hitler is said to be dead. Himmler cannot be found and Admiral Dönitz *(note: became head of state after Hitler's death)* has stated his intentions to continue the struggle and prolong the bloodshed until the bitter end.

But—Rotterdam may be used for reprovisioning purposes and one of our highroads has actually been used today for the conveyance of 1000 tons of food. Is not it glorious!

The next pages are meant to give you an idea of the news bulletins issued regularly by the illegal parties. The news for that day was very good and must not be looked upon as an average example. But I hope it may be interesting especially when read after my translation of the handbills put up by the authorities in Germany and Dutch a few days before about the same subject of bringing relief from the air.

3 May 1945

Bought 1kg. of leek for f. 3,50

10 heads of lettuce, 35 c. a head

And my salary presently is f 273.30

Two meals, warm meals a day. It's not easy to make both ends meet. And yet we did not pay too much attention to financial problems. For today the aeroplanes sent to bring us food came for the second time, some of them flying straight over our house.

We also heard that many trucks heavily loaded with victuals passed through Utrecht. They had come from No. Brabant. In large, sprawling letters they bore all sorts of encouraging inscriptions. Tilburg: Cheer up. It won't be long now. Den Bosch: Keep hearty, we soon hope to see you. Berlin fallen, Lübeck, Hamburg too.

Bernadotte *(note: Swedish foreign minister)* brought new proposals of capitulation from Himmler *(note: leader of the SS)*. Churchill expected to make an announcement in the House of Commons. Stockholm awaiting further important news to-day. To-day, Tuesday 1 May, is expected by the whole world to be a day of decisive importance. Reports from various sources, Allied as well as anemy and neutral, show that very important news may be expected at any rate. In London and not only there, the most contradictory reports are received. In one respect, however, they all agree: Count Bernadotte has been in contact again with Himmler at castle Abenra on the German-Danish frontier and that Himmler on this occasion has made new proposals of capitulation. After the interview Himmler returned to Lübeck where he is now waiting for a reply. Count Bernadotte was at Copenhagen yesterday evening where he was staying on his journey back to Sweden. Correspondents in Stockholm used the telephone to worm news out of him, but he refused to say anything. One correspondent, however, stated that he got the impression that the Count had been successful in his attempts, for he must have said: "I shall not return to Germany." It is generally expected in Stockholm that to-day will bring great news. In London and Washington, too, there is an atmosphere of high tension. Yesterday evening Churchill discussed (new?) proposals of capitulation from Himmler with several members of the Cabinet. In political circles it is believed that he may have something to say to the House to-day. Before the House of Commons meets to-day, the British Government will have another secret session. One of the regular speakers for the German wireless, Dr. Scharping, informed the German people yesterday evening that the war is drawing to a close. He spoke in the following words: "The turmoil of battle may go on for weeks, but it may stop to-morrow." And again the courage of the German soldier and the hard work, often implying great sacrifice, of the German woman have not been able to bring about the salvation of our country; not a word about Hitler, Himmler or one of the other great Nazi-leaders. The mystery about Hitler is still unsolved; it is rumoured that he is not in Berlin at all. An officer of high rank of the Swedish air force attached to the German army who had just left Berlin which is completely surrounded now, and has come back to Sweden, is said to have declared: "I have every reason to assume that Hitler is not in Berlin at all. From the beginning of the battle of Berlin I was in the capital of Germany, was continually in contact with the highest circles of command, but nobody ever saw a glimpse of Hitler." Others are of the opinion that Hitler died, that he was removed by Himmler and that his death will be made public together with the capitulation.

Again 1.250.000 KG of food for the Hague, Leyden, Rotterdam.

Yesterday Lancasters of the R.A.F. (have) once more dropped food above the Hague, Leyden and Rotterdam. This time 450 of these heavy bombers which from a height of 200 yards dropped 1250 tons of food, so more than twice as much as the day before yesterday, on the aviation field of Ypenburg and the race-course near Rotterdam; it was done in about $2\frac{1}{2}$ hours The Government issued the following official communication: the Dutch Government urgently appeals to all citizens in occupied territories strictly to follow all instructions which may promote a quick and just division of the food thrown down. It will be collected by Dutch officials, and then distributed in the normal way. The Government trusts that our citizens will maintain the necessary self-discipline, very difficult indeed and therefore the more necessary.

About the preparations for relief from the air the following things have been communicated: After five weeks of experimenting the plans were put to the test in the presence of officials of high rank in the British Ministry of War. The object was to pack the food in such a way that the inevitable damage might be as small as possible and to drop the packets when flying low exactly on the spot indicated. Among the crews they literally fought for places in the "food squadrons."

"The Dutch must have this food" was the motto.

München cleared. The Soviet-flag floating from the Reichstag. Morawska Ostrawa taken.

It has been stated officially that München is quite cleared now, Garmisch-Pertenkirchen and Mittenwald have been taken and the Americans are at 12 miles from Innsbrück. The 3rd Army on the Isar from Freising down to the confluence with the Danube and in three places across the Isar. The French seized on and near Lake Constanz, Friedrichshafen, Ravensburg, Lindau and are crossing the Austrian border near Bregenz. In Berlin the Soviet flag is floating from the building of the Reichstag and the General Post-Office; in the Wilhelmstrasze,

Dutchmen!

The Anglo-Americans announce their intention to drop small quantities of provisions from aeroplanes. They try to make the impression that this may be relief from starvation. In reality such quantities will never cover your lack of food. One single ship-load of 6000 tons would mean that one thousand heavily-laden aeroplanes would have to be poured out over your country. And then a ship-load too, would not at all be sufficient to alleviate your needs considerably.

Therefore the measures of the Anglo-Americans quoted above only and merely are propaganda-stunts.

The Supreme Command of the German Army in the Netherlands and the Governor for the occupied districts, on the other hand, have promised in principle to promote in an unselfish manner all attempts that may lead to a just division of food-transports among the Dutch population by the Dutch authorities. They have now proposed to the Chief-command of the Allied forces to organize transports by ship as they have been affected by the Red Cross together with transports from the provinces of Noord-Brabant and the provinces in the North East, in greater numbers and to a greater extent than has been done so far.

Only by such transports to an extent as desired by the German authorities, if allowed and promoted by the Anglo-Americans, a real help and a just division to all Dutchmen would be guaranteed so that not only a certain group of war profiteers should profit.

It is desirable if the Allies really are animated by good intentions that they shall agree to this support of the Dutch people. All other attempts of the Allies can only be looked upon as actions directed against German defence.

While the German troops would not use their weapons against 'planes flying low with the object to drop victuals, German transports, fortifications and other objects of military importance might be reconnoitred and attacked, parachutists might be let down, arms cast down and other actions might be prepared, injurious to the German army, the result of which might be that Dutch territory would unnecessarily be further destroyed.

For these reasons such hostile intentions must be prevented. Hunger is driven from your doors by actual help that ids doing everything to make transports by ship possible but not by propaganda stunts and secrete hostile actions.

The Governor of the
occupied Du.provinces

Tuesday, May 1 1945
Vrij Nederland Bulletin
Extra Number.
Nr. 145

A poster dated April 1945

Tiergarten, Unter den Linden and Kaiserhof they are still fighting desperately. Montgomery building two bridges across the lower course of the Elbe. Rokosowsky 60 miles W. of Stettin, approaching Stralsund and Rostock; Greifswald, Trentow, Neu-Strelitz taken. In Tjsecho-Slovakia Morawska Ostrawa, an important place, taken. General Marc Clark announces that the German army in Italy as a connected force has ceased to exist; the Allies are marching into Turin, Venice and Tito into Triest and Fiume. In three weeks time 120.000 prisoners in Italy, since D-day 2.628.000 in the West.

Latest news: According to Japan Radio landing of the Allies on the East coast of Borneo.

Do not put out your flag too soon.

If an official announcement of the capitulation should be published, people should wait showing the country's flag until the signal for this is given from public buildings or be allowed by official instances. Abstain from premature demonstration. Immediately after the official communication we hope to issue an extra bulletin.

A News-Bulletin
From the Liberation number of Trouw (= Loyalty)

A hearty welcome to you, soldiers of the Allied Armies.

Five years ago foreign troops overran our country. They came as usurpers and oppressors. We saw them walking through our streets and they lived in our houses. Now again foreign troops march along our canals and enter our houses. This time they have come as our friends, as our liberators.

And how welcome they are! All through these long, dark years we have waited for you. We knew that one day you would come and give us back the freedom we have lacked so sorely. Now that you have bravely fought your way to us and the Grand Day of our liberation has come, we only want to say: Thank you with all our heart. We hope you will have a good time in our country and enjoy the real Dutch hospitality. Of course you may count upon our help, wherever you want it. God bless you all.

± 1975

Dramatis personae
Grandfather (that's me)
Grandson (as yet unborn)

Gramps: Well, my little fellow, and now your wishes for your birthday. Come and sit on my knee and let me hear them.

Grands: Please, Grandfather, could I have some tanks? You know the kind I have seen at Charley's house. They can take the steepest slope, drive into the water like submarines and when he turns a handle, up they go into the air as high as the ceiling of his room. And then, let me see, yes, a picture-book full of pups and ponies and horses and rabbits, of course. And a sailing-boat with three masts. You could not get one with four, could you? And a new pencil, a big one, red at one end and blue at the other. And, well, there's lots of other things I should like to have but, grandfather, the tanks, don't you think they are the best. The sort that can fly, you know.

Gramps: I'll tell you. But you better sit down beside me because you are getting heavy and it's rather a long story. Many, many years ago when your father was a little boy like you—oh, no, that's wrong—when he was a fine big boy as you are now, we lived in a little village right in the centre of Holland. One morning we were all in bed and dreaming of Christmas puddings as big as houses. We woke with a start because a great many 'planes were buzzing over our heads. They would not frighten you, because you see them every day and I hear you often help Daddy when he takes out the 'plane in the morning to go to his work. But in those days we only saw them once or twice a week and we would run out of the house, point them out to each other and shout: " Oh, that's a big one" or " How fast it goes!"

And on that particular morning the sky was full of them, hundreds and hundreds. They had come from Germany and we soon learned that they would do the very wickedest things if we did not allow the German soldiers to pass though our country. But our Queen—we had a queen then—would not hear of it. She said to them: "This is our country and nobody is allowed to come here if we don't like it." And of course we did not like to see foreign soldiers in our villages and towns with rifles, machine-guns and tanks.

And then the Germans said: You'd better think it over. For if you try to prevent us passing through these provinces, we'll shoot as hard as we can and we'll tell the pilots of our 'planes to swoop down on your towns and drop bombs on them. We had not done anything to make them angry, so our Queen would not, could not believe what they had said and she ordered our soldiers to drive them out of the country again if they dared to cross our frontiers. And then they began to fight. Our soldiers did their best, but if you have been quarreling with two other boys and you come to blows, I'm sure you could easily knock them down. Three too, perhaps, if you had had a good breakfast and if you didn't sneeze or hiccough when you were half way but what about ten or twenty? Then you would certainly have a bleeding nose or worse before you had had time to begin in good earnest. And the Germans came in thousands, hundreds of thousands, some say in millions.

We would not give in, though. Then they did bomb one of our towns. That was so terrible, houses burnt down, people killed that our Government said after five days: This can't go on. They might destroy all of our towns and kill many more men, women and children. So we had to let them pass through our country, but the other nations who had tried to help us were very angry with them when they heard what the Germans had done to us and they put their hands on the Bible and said: God, will you be on our side in this war against those cruel Nazis—that was what we called the Germans when we were in a bad temper.

This war soon spread to nearly all the countries of Europe. And everywhere people were killed and beautiful churches were burnt down and fine football fields and cricket pitches were turned into aviation-grounds.

Your father could not go to school any more. At first he was very glad for he was just doing vulgar fractions—it was the fourth form—and vulgar fractions are awfully difficult. But he soon found out that chopping wood every day and gathering dead branches every week and getting wet feet because the shoemaker had no leather to repair the soles was far worse than going to school. And when this terrible war went on there came a time that we could not give him enough food, we only got one and a half bread in a whole week. That's not much for three persons. And he often looked at us after carefully scraping his plate until you could not see that he had eaten from it as if he would say: "What a pity, isn't it. I'm sure my stomach is not half full yet." But your father was a brave little fellow and never said anything about it. But I remember quite well that he had made a list of things he wanted to have on his tenth birthday. What do you think he put at the top? When the war is over, the 12th of May, please can I have half a pound of butter? Now, what do you think of that? Butter as a present on your birthday?

That was all because of this horrible war. I could tell you much more about it. How our house was blown up, how your father often ran home as fast as he could when he heard 'planes that might begin to shoot at any moment, how cold we were without a nice fire because we had no coal.

But I will only say that this war was like a huge, black monster with strong hands taking right and left what he could get and trampling under his huge, hob-nailed boots a great many things that were nice and pretty, red and blue and green and yellow before he came and grey and withered or dull and dark and dead after he had passed.

This is not a nice story, Peter, but it all really happened many years ago exactly as I have told you. After five years of war people gradually got sick of it and they said: Can't we kill this huge, black monster? If millions and millions of people say: We will even a great monster can't do much against them. And then the war stopped. But we could not remove the crosses on the graves of the soldiers who had fallen and we could not restore to life the children who had been burned and many of us had quite forgotten how to laugh and be cheerful. They only found out or rather remembered how this is done long and long after that. Because the guns on the land, the 'planes in the air and the submarines at sea had done their work very, very thoroughly. And—the tanks, Peter. Yes, I must not forget the tanks.

I shall do my best for you, little man, but you must not be angry with me if I can't give you some tanks on your birthday.

Grands: That's right, Grampa. A big, brown pencil would be very fine, too. But four colours, don't forget.

Capitulation and Deliverance!

Today, May 4th in the evening, the Supreme command of the Allies announced, that the German armies in Holland and N.W. Germany and Denmark have capitulated, this including Helgoland and the North-Frisian inlands, so not Norway. The capitulation will become effective this morning at 8 o'clock. They surrendered to field marshall Montgomery.

The treaty was signed Friday evening at half past six. The Prime Minister, Mr. Gerbrandy, will speak on the wireless, Radio Oranje, at one o'clock this afternoon.

It is quite beyond me to give utterance to the feelings that over-whelmed us on Friday evening at about 9 o'clock when this was made public. The following Sunday Thanksgiving-services were held in all churches. Let me use the text of the vicar on this memorable day to conclude this short survey which I introduced with the words – "When Ruin's wheel rolled o'er us."

The words are found in Psalm 124:

> (If it had not been the Lord who was on our side; now may
> Israel say;)
> If it had not been the Lord who was on our side, when men
> rose up against us:
> Then they had swallowed us up quick, when their wrath was
> kindled against us:
> Then the waters had overwhelmed us, the stream had gone
> over our soul:
> Then the proud waters had gone over our soul.
> Blessed be the Lord, who hath not given us as a prey to their
> teeth.
> Our soul is escaped as a bird out of the snare of the fowlers:
> The snare is broken, and we are escaped
> Our help is in the name of the Lord, who made heaven and
> earth.

Bussum, 6 May 1945
the day when the capitulation was signed at Hilversum.

A free man in a free country

"Befehl ist Befehl." That was the current phrase the Germans used to intimate there was nothing for it but obey—"Order is Order." And this Monday, the 7th of May 1945, our headmaster had told us that it was his intention to resume lessons for the highest forms. Final examinations might be held, also in this fifth year of war. He could not have foreseen when the porter was sent around with this news that this very Monday would be the day on which it was utterly impossible to think of anything else than the arrival of the Canadians, our liberators.

So I took my bike, the war bike. You know the sort?

Solid tyres, creaking wherever a machine consisting of steel, far from stainless, of iron very rusty, a machine that has not seen grease or oil for years, can creak. The chain stubbornly refused to remain where it ought to be for more than two or three miles. And yet, how useful the vehicles were, how dear they were to us, what tales they would have to tell if they could only speak.

I took my bike and went cheerfully and noisily schoolward. Was there a house without our national colours? No. Did I see one man, one woman or a single child without flag, cockade, an orange scarf, or red, white and blue tie? No. Was there a pupil at the entrance of the building where we as a school had resided for the past few years? Of course not.

And I went on. And into the country. To Laren and Blaricum. Where I saw the yellow buttercups and the blue speedwell, the gold of the furze on the heath and the russet leaves of oak trees just out. The young corn, half a yard high, had donned its brightest green and the blackbird was singing in the birches. And the colours were more beautiful, the song of the bird more melodious, the odours of a fine morning in spring better than ever before.

In the villages the men of the illegal parties were taking up their various positions to maintain order. Young men in blue overalls, many of them with hollow cheeks and deep lines in their faces. But marching proudly in military fashion, one or two with rifles, in front and at the back. A man took off his hat as they passed and I fell a lump in my throat.

Then on again. Through the woods where wide gaps had been left after the last terrible winter. Across the heath where shelters and dug-outs were lying deserted. Along the road where the last bombs of our friends had destroyed houses and hotels to drive out the oppressors.

But the young trees will be planted, and the dug-outs will be leveled and covered up with green and the ruins will be removed.

For we are Dutchman, are not we? We are a nation that wrested its fertile provinces from the sea, a nation that fought eighty years to gain that inestimable property called liberty and we are all full of youthful vigour to begin again.

And after the villages and after the country back into the little town again. Just in time to see them. Only eight or ten tanks and armoured cars. But a whole army could not have raised more enthusiasm.

Here I am, sitting in my garden—the English 'planes are now and then passing over my head. Still throwing down their packets of food. The flags of the neighbouring houses are floating—orange red and white against the blue of the sky.

And I hear a full-throated melodious voice: Is it Pippa passing? I seem to hear:

God's in his Heaven, all's right with the world.[14]

Aftermath

8 May 1945

I can't stop yet. Fortunately these notes were never meant to form a book, introductory chapters, denouement, development of the plot, climax, concluding chapters, happy end. I can go on if the right mood sticks to me.

This morning we rose at six. At half past I was on my bike again. When I told you about the 10th of May 1940, I told you something of what happened to us at Soest, a little village not far from Utrecht. It was there that we turned the key in the lock of the front door not knowing if we were to find back again what had become dear to us in earthly goods. It was there that we came back after a fortnight and had lunch at the house of a neighbour facing our own, our house that had not suffered in those five days of war. And all through these years we had said to each other: When it is over, we shall go to Soest. That's the best place to congratulate one another that a new leaf is going to be turned over.

And therefore at half past six on my bike to see if our best friends there could have us on the following Sunday? I did not get far. After I had left the last houses behind me, I soon came upon half a dozen men of the reserve-police force. They told me that the high roads, byroads and paths were guarded. Nobody without a special permit was allowed to pass. They had been hunting down members of the N.S.B. the day before. Some of them were still hiding or trying to escape. In order to make flight practically impossible for them, they had had to take this measure. Unpleasant for a man who had written the day before a chapter bearing the proud title: A free man in a free country.

But I knew that doing justice to those who had been unworthy of the name of Dutchmen in the pat years, was one of those things that had to be carried out. Therefore no grumbling, no protests. I went home again. First to the greengrocer. See if he had anything that was not too great a tax on my financial resources.

A short bulletin of the illegal, now very legal, paper: Vrijheid (Liberty) stating that regrettable incidents in Amsterdam had made some hundred of victims. People had assembled at the Dam, a square that's better known and of greater historical significance to a Dutchman than Trafalgar Square to an Englishman., the square where one side is taken up by the Royal Palace, where one has a view of the Exchange, of the New Church, the burying place of Admiral de Ruyter *(note: famous admiral from beginning of Dutch Republic era).*

And naturally the Amsterdammer goes there at times of national rejoicing, all great ceremonies take place there. We may imagine that these days, too, thousands of them went there to witness the arrival of the British troops. Grüne Polizei *(note: German police)* came, threw hand-grenades and they made victims. The German authorities have expressed their regret. Excuse? The men were drunk.

In Utrecht, Dordrecht, Rotterdam similar incidents are said to have taken place.

The word of welcome to those who liberated us, on another stenciled sheet made better reading.

"In the name of the population of our cities and towns we call you welcome, allied soldiers. You bring us the freedom we have been looking forward to for so many years and for which many of our comrades gave up their lives. In silent respect we think of your comrades who fell for our common cause.

This moment of liberty makes us hope that the sufferings we have gone through together may form the foundation for a peaceful contact of the free nations in the new world."

At the corner I hear two men speaking in a rather loud voice. One gives utterance to his discontent, the other is almost violent in his protestations that words to that effect at this moment are unforgivable. At the greengrocer's shop the usual long queue. Five kilos of red beet for every customer—I take my place at the tail end. And after half an hour I have my ration. And yesterday the milkman came at the door, and he had 1 l. of unadulterated milk for us. Let us hope that the new, or rather, the old authorities who have been appointed to their former posts, will not forget the very important problem of provisioning. In the first moments we forgot everything, but people are still hungry and the packets with the valuable contents must bring rapid relief for there are many of is who cannot hold out much longer.

To the old city of Naarden now. Where the inhabitants have also done their best to decorate their old houses, to match the narrow, winding streets, one unbroken line of gratitude in colour.

Another proclamation.

The burgomaster denounces all continuation of the "so called" black trade. Those who are found to go on asking exorbitant prices, buyer as well as seller, will be subject to severe penalties and their names will be put up for pillory.

Will this be more effective than the words in our press columns of yesterday?

And now home again. At one of the schools a great number of German soldiers are assembling. They have left them their weapons. But all the cars have already disappeared, the horses, taken from the Dutch farmers and carriers, are unharnessed, and the faces of the men are so many silent symbols of the collapse of Nazi Germany

At three o'clock I heard Big Ben. And the old crystal of the primitive wireless set of 25 years ago brought the words of Mr. Winston Churchill, short, matter-of-fact, English.

Winding up with: Advance Brittania—Long live the cause of Freedom. God Save the King.

9 May 1945: The Way to Recovery

At 9 o'clock yesterday evening I heard King George VI, speaking to his people. Words of gratitude—less matter-of-fact. More heart-to-heart than the Prime Minister, words of prayer to Him who had given us this day of victory and whose guiding hand we should want in the future as we had found it in the past. "God save the King" at the end more impressive than I have ever heard it before.

The King sent the following message to Queen Wilhelmina:

"At long last your country has been liberated. Together with my people and the whole world I have followed with increasing solicitude the terrible sufferings of your subjects and admired the stubborn courage with which they continued to offer resistance to the enemy. I and my government are glad that we have been able to give hospitality to Your Majesty and the Dutch Government and to all who formed part of the Dutch forces that distinguished themselves so honorably on the battle field."

And all this with a primitive wireless set with a crystal as we used 25 years ago.

This morning the troops arrived that will be garrisoned in our town during these days of transition. Young men who have come all the way from Canada to destroy the powers of evil that were threatening to ruin civilized life in Europe. In two schools that had been hastily prepared for their reception. My son who had been in bed with dysentery for some days and had missed the arrival of the "Tommies" ran away and came back again waving a precious bit of paper. "Father, father!!!" What can one do with three marks of exclamation to give an idea of the bubbling excitements in these words: "Look here." "The signature of a Canadian soldier of the British Expeditionary Forces." "Gordon Snow!" "Grand, isn't it."

"Yes, it is. Just fine."

On my morning tour I found the boy-scouts, girl-guides energetically scrubbing, sweeping, dusting in their old buildings, with evident pleasure on their beaming faces. All traces of the former occupants, de Jeugdstorm, youth organization of the N.S.B. had to be removed.

In the windows of several shops a proclamation of the Queen, and an order of the day from Prince Bernhard to all the men of the illegal parties or underground organizations. The men in the blue overalls have been sent out with means of conveyance of the most variegated kinds for food. And their activity is beginning to show. To-morrow my wife may go to the grocer who has been distributing the Red Cross packets and she may come back with:

One whole loaf
750 gr. of beans or peas
150 gr. of sugar per head.

That's something. And the local authorities have promised that the food that is prepared by the Central kitchens, will improve in quality and quantity. This time, with other men at the helm, promises may be kept. It will be easy to see the result of their work. For I had myself weighed this morning. 71.7 kg. And my length is 1.86m. According to the lists generally put up somewhere on these weighing-machines it ought to be 86kg. Only 15 kg. short. There are many who are in worse condition.

Everywhere in town the first signs that work is being resumed after some days of rejoicing. Shops are open again, people have put on their working clothes. I drop in at the bookseller's. Peter, who's going to celebrate his tenth birthday has asked me if he could get a couple of pencils, pre-war quality. And the shops-assistant says: "Yes, I have. It's Faber, made in Germany. But it will do." Well, as long as it is restricted to pencils and similar things, it does not matter.

But I do hope we shall not make the same mistakes as in 1914-'18 again, the attitude which made Piscator whom I quoted at the beginning of these notes, write: Is it Shakespeare only, Rousseau only, Goethe only, Tolstoy only, who gave the whole world something that will outlast a few more generations, or did they all give us something for which we, and our children and our grandchildren after that will be grateful.

Are we not going to play Beethoven any more, no Schiller at our schools, no German knives on our tables and no German water through our Rhine?

That would be too bad.

We shall go on sawing and cutting wood for our smoking emergency stoves, we shall go on sweeping the floors with dustpan and brush and we shall fetch our water from the pump of our neighbour just a little longer, but the gas-stove will be restored, the vacuum-cleaner will become active and the tap will be ready for use at all hours of day and night again.

And long after the names of Hitler, of Goebbels *(note: Hiler's prop-
aganda minister)*, Himmler, Von Ribbentrop *(note: Hitler's foreign min-
ister)*, and the rest will be forgotten,
 "Das Lied von der Glocke" will be read in our schools,
 Goethe's Faust will be studied and Bach's music
 Will be heard in our churches to the Glory of God.

Ascension Day

To-day's news says that Göring has been taken prisoner. And
Quisling, the man from Norway, Degrelle, the Belgian Fascist, and Mr.
Seyss Inquart.

How Mussert was seized.

By four members of the Binnenlandse Strijdkrachten, Netherlands
Home Forces. To all appearance dignified and calm he declared:

I am at your disposal. At the moment of the unexpected raid the
"Leader" of the Dutch people was just partaking of a large dish of
strawberries. The commanding officer declared that it was advisable
to bring food for 24 hours. In this house is no food, the man assured
who has often said that without National Socialism Holland wants
have no future. He then was allowed to finish his meal before he was
led away.

My neighbour over the way had his first talk with one of the boys
from Canada. He had signed as a volunteer at the outbreak of the war,
so he had had five years of it. Italy had been his worst time. One out
of five had been killed in their ranks there. There was not much hatred
of the Germans in him, but a very pronounced dislike of the English. I
hope it is not the general opinion amongst them. He went as far as calling Mr. Winston Churchill " the Old pig." There must be some ideal-
ism, or inbred aversion against terrorism or oppression if one wants to
understand that after all those years in Africa, in Italy, in France, they
have signed again to be be of those who are preparing for the final struggle against Japan.

On the highroad to Amsterdam the first signs that civilian traffic is
coming to life again. At the wheels men in working-clothes or in their
Sunday best and not always khaki. The German traffic-boards in yellow and black are replaced by others with English directions. There is
a motor-car with trailer parked on the berm from Steenwijk in the
North East of our country. The chauffeur may have brought potatoes

or flour to Amsterdam. On his windscreen no longer the German word 'Währung' but "food-supply."

But the milkman still charges £2/6 for 2 pints of milk; price before the war tuppence. I hear that the illegal forces are going to put their foot down to stop it. At the entrance to the church I find a short notice: On Sunday next divine service will be held in Dutch and in English. And on Monday all the youth organizations will join for a march past at the station to pay tribute to the solidarity and stubborn resistance of all the railway-employees during the long months of their strike.

The first ships have arrived in Rotterdam. 3000 tons of food and coal. And how indispensable these imports will be for some time to be. It is said that just now we can cover only 20% of our wants with all that has been left to us by the Germans.

Perhaps Amsterdam will be used too. I hear that one of the harbours is not damaged, and that one of locks at Ijmuiden can still be used.

In the immediate surroundings of the two schools occupied by the Canadians men of the underground organization stand guard. The cordial welcome of the Dutch people, especially of the Dutch girls, knows no bounds and might become too much for those who have been hardened by war.

And at this very moment my wife returns with the first result of the activity of our new authorities to whom the provisioning of the starved or half-starved has been entrusted.

400 gr. of bread, 750 gr. of peas and 150 gr. of sugar for each of us.

The weather remains fine and our flags are still floating.

"Holland Free Again"

Holland, with your snow-white seagulls
    And your dunes in sparkling light,
With your sailors and your farmers
    All these men that know no fright.
With your water, wood and fen –
    Holland, Holland free again

Holland, how your flags are streaming
  O'er the heads of happy men.
And the sun is brightly beaming
  On your red, white blue again.
Grief and slavery from your door –
  Holland, Holland free once more.
Holland, let us praise the soldiers
  Who came in our hour of need,
Who have grimly fought their way
  To us with memorable deed.
Let us sing to those brave men:
  Thank you, Holland's free again

For the above poem I am greatly indebted to: Willem v. Iependaal who wrote: "Holland is Weer Vrij."

It was published by F.G. Kroonder-Bussum and could be seen in the place of honour on the very day that the capitulation was ratified, in many of our book and music shops.

It seemed best to give the impression of the great event so shortly after the last incidents in the very heart of our capital in the words of a Canadian War Correspondent. We heard that their reception in Paris, Brussels or Antwerp was as nothing compared to the excitement they saw here. It is easy enough to account for it. We had sunk far deeper, our need was far greater than in those countries that were delivered from tyranny at an earlier date.

One of these days we may also hear the voice of John Steinbeck, the well-known writer of *The Grapes of Wrath*. He is one of the war correspondents who came with the troops to Amsterdam. But we have plenty of boys here now who are willing to quench our thirst for reliable news after all these years of a questionable press. The first question that is nearly always asked of them is: "And are you not glad it's over now." Is not it remarkable that it is only seldom that we hear an emphatic "Yes" or Rather!" from these young men. They never for a moment seem to forget that Japan has not been beaten yet. An officer said that even then the war might not be over for them. "What then?" they asked him. "First Japan, then Russia, and last, very probably, though not quite certain, against England, for a Canada that is really free." Can there be some truth in the fact that we often heard

---

The Canadians arrive in Amsterdam

"A great day."

This day of liberation of Amsterdam will be forever memorable to Canadian troops. The regiments who entered our city, the Seaforth Highlanders of Canada, the Princess Patricia's Canadian Light Infantry, the Loyal Edmonton Regiment have fought up length and breadth of Italy, but they have never known such a day as this.

We know what dark nightmare has been lifted from your hearts and minds. While Germans would in the end have been driven from Holland regardless of any decision which Blaskowitz (note: Colonel-General Johannes Blaskowitz) could make, most of us feared that country would be ravaged by grimmest kind of war before freedom was secure again.

Now as if by a miracle your dreads and ours are banished for ever and you have expressed your joy in rousing demonstrations that literally swept us off our feet and off our jeeps.

Nothing that has happened in this war more incensed the people of Canada and the United States than and the wanton and brutal German attack on the Netherlands whose people are so much like us in many ways.

This is a great day for freedom and I hope it will usher in a new ear of peace and progress, for a country which we have always admired for its proud achievements in culture, science, art and social relations.

Long live the friendship of the Netherlands and the Dominion of Canada in loyalty to common ideals of the United Nations."

Maurice Western,
Winnipeg Free Press.

---

that the soldiers from the Dominion were sent by the English to the most dangerous spots, that the most difficult jobs were given to them and that this method has created ill-feeling, in some cases ill-concealed dislike?

I am not the only one who wants to give his English friends some idea of these years of decline and resurrection. The other day I met the president of the 'Militair Tehuis' (Military Home). "If you are trying to find people who can do something in the evening for our guests, I am at your disposal" I said. "They may be interested to hear something about our experiences. I wrote down something to make use of when it will be possible to go to England again." "So did I," he said.

A friend dropped by and said: "Can you help me? An acquaintance has written something about these great days. He'll have it translated into French, English and wants suitable mottos or slogans to introduce these sessions for our Allied friends."

I set to work and suggested among others:

> Wake: the silver dusk returning
>   Up the beach of darkness brims,
> And the ship of sunrise burning
>   Strands upon the eastern rims.
>
> Wake: the vaulted shadow shatters,
>   Trampled to the floor it spanned,
> And the tent of night in shatters
>   Straws the sky-pavilioned land

From: Alfred Edward Housman, "Reveille"

What I am feeling, but could not possibly express, is perhaps best approached in:

"Sunday" by James Thomson

> Let my voice ring out and over the earth,
> Through all the grief and strife,
>   With a golden joy in a silver mirth:
> Thank God for Life!
> Let my voice swell out through the great abyss
>   To the azure dome above,
> With a chord of faith in the harp of bliss:
>   Thank God for Love!
>
> Let my voice thrill out beneath and above
>   The whole world through:
> O my Love and Life, O my Life and Love,
>   Thank God for you!

The following passage from Swinburne's "Atalanta in Calydon" also reflects much of our thoughts and feelings:

> For winter's rains and ruins are over,
>   And all the season of snows and sins:
> The days dividing lover and loser,
>   The light that loses, the night that wins;
> And time remembered is grief forgotten,
> And frosts are slain and flowers begotten,
> And in green underwood and cover
>   Blossom by blossom the spring begins.

And then all of a sudden the beautiful rhythmic beat of Tennyson's "In Memoriam" came upon me and it is not impossible that on the fly-leaf of the book the following words will be printed:

> Ring out the years of care and sin
> And ancient forms of party strife:
> Now for a nobler, happy life
> With work for all, let's ring that in.

Whitsun

When I am asked to give advice about a correct pronunciation of English, I generally tell my pupils: Go to church or to the theatre and you may be sure that you will learn something. And now, after five years of broken connections, we have plenty of opportunities to hear English again, unfortunately not always of a kind to recommend as a trustworthy guide for pronunciations. For our Canadian friends have an unmistakable American accent. Would it be the same with educated people, with servants of the Church? On Whitsunday I went to our Spieghelkerk, where the chaplain held divine services for his soldiers at nine o'clock but Dutch civilians were heartily welcome.

The men in khaki—especially the older ones I noticed—on the left hand of the pulpit, the Dutch guests on the right.

The army chaplain proved to be the right shepherd for the flock. Did not I tell you that the boys we had at our schools, were all broad-shouldered, heavily built, fine men? Their chaplain was a worthy representative of the country that sent us such remarkably good things as bacon, chopped pork, condensed milk and chocolate. One could not possibly say whether he had any yoke-bones, where his chin terminated and his throat began, but he had a fine voice and his delivery when reading the appropriate text from the Acts of the Apostles, the second chapter, was a treat in itself.

1. And when the day of Pentecost was fully come, they were all with one accord in one place.
2. And suddenly there came a sound from heaven as of a rushing mighty wind, and it filled all the house where they were sitting.
3. And there appeared unto them dozen tongues like as of fire, and it sat upon each of them.
4. And they were all filled with the Holy Ghost, and began to speak with other tongues, as the Spirit gave them utterance.
5. And there were dwelling at Jerusalem Jews, devout men, out of every nation under heaven.
6. Now when this was noised abroad, the multitude came together, and were confounded, because that every man heard them speak in his own language.
7. And they were all amazed and marveled, saying one to another, Behold, are not all these which speak Galilaeans?
8. And how hear we every man in our own tongue, wherein we were born?
12. And they were all amazed were in doubt, saying one to another, what meaneth this?
13. Others mocking said: These men are full of new wine.
14. But Peter, standing up with the eleven, lifted up his voice, and aid unto them, Ye men of Judaea, and all ye that dwell at Jerusalem, be this known unto you, and hearken to my words:
15. For these are not drunken, as ye suppose, seeing it is but the third house of thy day.
16. But this is that which was spoken to the prophet Joel;
17. And it shall come to pass in the last days, Faith God, I will pour out my spirits upon all flesh: and your sons and your daughters shall prophesy, and your young men shall see visions, and your old men shall dream dreams:

18. And on my servants and on my handmaidens I will pour
    out in those days of my Spirit; and they shall prophesy;
19. And I will shew wonders in heavens above, and signs in the
    earth beneath; Blood, and fire, and vapour of smoke:
20. The sun shall be turned into darkness, and the moon into
    blood, before that great day of the Lord come:
21. And it shall come to pass, that whoever shall call on the
    name of the Lord shall be saved.

The clergyman opened with the singing of our national anthem,
hymn number 83 may be the national song in Canada—I must
inquire—and with a "God save the King" the service was concluded.

It seems that everything we see and hear these days will be remembered for ever after. For we live a life of strong impressions—and many
things which seemed common place yesterday assume new significance.
The most striking example of this is found in fine words and beautiful
music of the old songs as found in "Valerius Gedenckklank." It is only
now that we understand the words of the poet and the deeply religious
or martial music of the composer of these days of the Eighty Years' War
fully—now that our hearts and minds have become responsive to these
voices of another time of struggle, oppression, sorrow, hardship, followed by ultimate relief.

In the afternoon we went to Soest, the village where we intended
to go some days before. Now the barriers put up between one district
and another, have been removed again and we could carry out our plan.
It was a good, a very good day. Our acquaintances were in the best of
spirits. Fancy, three children in the war or mixed up with it in such a
way that their lives might be at stake, and all three safe and well.

Son-in-law, living at New York, has been with the Canadian army
for over two years, suddenly dropped out of the air and said: Here I am.
How are you? He had read an advertisement in an American paper that
the son in the Du. East Indies had married, and he brought the happy
news that the eldest who had been removed to a concentration camp in
Germany had survived this ordeal and was doing well, working as an
interpreter in Belgium for the repatriation of Belgians and Frenchmen
from Germany.

We sang: Holland's free again—with all our hearts.

Also in honor of the third son, who had done illegal work for quite a long time and who had been chosen as the right man to welcome the first Canadians who came to Laren, that romantic, picturesque village in our Gooi-district but in those days of war one of the most thoroughly hated strongholds of passive and very often active resistance.

Coda

I will be brief about my father's stories you have just read. I don't need to put myself between him and the reader with a lengthy analysis, and I don't think much purpose is served from the armchair perspective of the post-war generation. It was what it was, and it clearly was quite awful in many ways. In my judgment, my parents maintained their decency in the war, and that is a gift.

My father's stories put to rest any notion that war, especially for non-combatants, is anything but hell. I may add that, during the twentieth century, the ratio between non-combatant deaths and combatant deaths has dramatically changed. In the vast carnage of World War II and other wars, civilian deaths outstrip the deaths among soldiers by a very wide margin.

Clearly, all the usual clichés apply: freedom, peace and democracy are notions we always under-appreciate until they are gone.

When I read my father's stories for the first time I was surprised that there is not a word about that pivotal incident when my parents argued whether to hide a Jewish girl. Was my father uncomfortable with the hindsight knowledge that his rational assessment in smelling the trap for what it was somehow did not measure up to the pure, "in the moment:" instinct of my mother to rescue the girl? We will never know, although my father's judgment saved the family and made it possible for me to exist. This macabre dance on the moral fault line haunts me still today.

I am puzzled that my father writes so little about his wife and my brother Piet. They appear, but mostly in neutral coloration; they are not fully sketched. Was that so because the occupation was the story, not the family per se? Was this just typical of his generation which did not "let it all hang out" as we would say decades later? Or did the war, and the emasculation of his sense of self and autonomy just feed his tendency toward depression and its accompanying feeling of being lonely, though not alone? I do not have an answer to these questions either.

But I do remember that my late brother once said to me that he thought my parents lived in constant fear during the war. I did not believe it then. I do believe it now. For instance, the uncertainly how long a permit exempting my father from forced labor would be in force must have been terrifying. When you read his story of the *razzia* you get a sense of that.

I had heard about the hunger winter of 1944-45, as you know, but until I read my father's story on foraging for food, I realized I had never fully understood the dire straits of those months. You now know he became obsessed with food. Of course, millions of parents in the third world face that obsession with food and starvation every day. How utterly desperate must it feel to look into the eyes of your child when you don't know how to feed it.

True, in our world it is no longer just the man who is supposed to be the bread winner, the sold provider, or head of household. But in my father's days, the culture was different and I have nothing but profound sympathy for his utter sense of diminishment when the family is on the edge of starvation. But he gathers himself and goes on his trip through snow, sleet and ice in his desperate search for help. Later, he could not even do that anymore because of new *razzia* and it fell to my mother to go on these hunts. I hold my parents in deep respect for these foraging trips: I think they were brave and noble.

I also feel deep affection for my father when he writes about his frustration with the erosion of Dutch Language, culture and values under occupation, because he was such a cultured man, and that fact is at the core of his legacy to me. He describes how Dutch society lost its decency during the war. It is a biting commentary and provides, of course, another insight into the abandonment of that society's Jews.

As we now say farewell to my father and his stories, we turn to a core issue: genocide often happens under conditions of warfare, not just in and by itself. Therefore, in the third part of this book, we will examine the roots of genocide in some detail.

My father in the early 1950s.

My mother in the early 1950s.

Drawing as therapy during war: my father draws his son Piet.

Dad draws a war dog (but not a German shepherd).

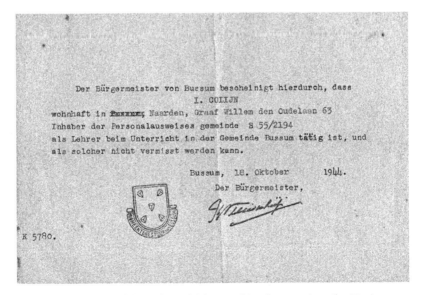

Receipt from the Nazi mayor of Amsterdam: Dad has signed the "Aryan declaration"—he is not a Jew.

Temporary relief from forced labor and/or deportation: the Nazi mayor of Bussum issues an exemption to my father on the grounds that he is an indispensable teacher.

I.Colijn
Gr.W. de Oudelaan 63

LASTGEVING

De Burgemeester van Naarden vordert U hierbij in opdracht van de Wehrmachtkommandantur Hilversum om bewakingsdiensten te verrichten op den Rijksweg en wel op het gedeelte, gelegen tusschen K.M.paal *18,6* en K.M.paal *20,6*, in het etmaal, aanvangende op *15* September 1944, te 20 uur, en eindigende op *16* September 1944, eveneens te 20 uur.

Uwe diensttijden staan hieronder vermeld. De te verstrekken witte armbanden, moeten aan den opvolger worden overgedragen. U mag Uw post niet verlaten, alvorens Uw opvolger den dienst heeft overgenomen.

U moet verhinderen, dat op het door U te bewaken gedeelte van den Rijksweg, glasscherven, spijkers of andere voorwerpen, welke gevaar voor het verkeer opleveren, gestrooid worden. Bij het aantreffen van dergelijke voorwerpen moeten deze onmiddellijk worden verwijderd. Indien zulks niet tijdig gelukt, zijn naderende voertuigen overdag door armzwaaien tot stilstand te brengen.

Niet opvolging van dit bevel wordt als sabotage aangemerkt; als repressaille zullen huizen in brand worden gestoken.

NAARDEN, *15* September 1944.
De Burgemeester voornoemd,
~~JUR. VISSER Jr.~~, wnd.
T. K. Buikenhuis.

A	B	C
20—22 uur	22—24 uur	24— 2 uur
2— 4 uur	4— 6 uur	6— 8 uur
8—10 uur	10—12 uur	12—14 uur
14—16 uur	16—18 uur	18—20 uur

AFLOSSING MOET GESCHIEDEN BIJ KILOMETERPAAL 20,6 (KRUISPUNT THIERENSWEG - RIJKSWEG)

K 1900

One of many Nazi orders for civil guard duty: an order to protect the highway from sabotage.

VEREENIGING
„SCHOOL VOOR VOORBEREI-
DEND HOOGER-, MIDDELBAAR-
EN MAATSCHAPPELIJK ONDER-
WIJS" TE BUSSUM.

Secretariaat:
Naarderstraat 306 - Huizen (N.-H.)

Postrekening 77561 } Bussum
Telefoon 5766 }

LYCEUM TE BUSSUM

Bussum, 29 Januari 1945.

Der Stellvertretende Rektor des
Lyceums zu Bussum erklärt:
dass J. Colijn, Oberlehrer an ten-
genannter Schule ist;
dass sein Haus am 30ten November
1944 bombardiert worden ist, bei welchem
viele seiner Eigentümmer verloren gegangen
sind, auch seine wenigen kostbaren Lebens-
mittel.
Ich habe das Obige in Betracht genommen
und ihm Urlaub gegeben nach Venhuizen
in West-Friesland zu gehen, wo er Freunde
hat, die im Stande sind ihm zu helfen.

Stellvertretender Rektor.

Dad gets an affidavit that the family home has been
bombed with   permission to go north in search of food

Het Amsterdamsch Lyceum
_____

Aan de gehuwde Docenten en aan het
gehuwde personeel van Het Amsterdamsch
Lyceum.
_____

Het Departement van Opvoeding, Wetenschap en Kultuurbescherming be-
richt ons, evenals aan de andere bijzondere gymnasia, lycea, hogere
burgerscholen, enz. bij circulaire No.13908, afdeling V.H.M.O. dd.
26 Augustus 1942 het volgende:

"Op last van den Rijkscommissaris voor het bezette Nederlandsche
gebied dient een lijst te worden samengesteld van alle ambtenaren en
het overig personeel in 's Rijks dienst,
gehuwd met een persoon, die volgens paragraaf 4 der Verordening Nr.
198/1940 betreffende het aangeven van ondernemingen, Jood is of als
zoodanig moet worden beschouwd. In die lijst dienen mede te worden
opgenomen degenen, die in dienst zijn van een provincie, van een gemeente of van een ander publiekrechtelijk lichaam of van een zoodanig
privaatrechtelijk lichaam, waaraan het Rijk, een provincie, een gemeente of een ander publiekrechtelijk lichaam deelneemt, benevens
degenen, die een eereambt bekleeden, alsmede alle personen, die aan
een bijzondere school zijn verbonden.
Ten einde aan deze opdracht te kunnen voldoen, verzoek ik U mij vóór
10 September a.s. een opgave, als hiervoren bedoeld, betreffende het
personeel van Uw school (scholen) en de leden van Uw bestuur te doen
toekomen. Ook negatieve opgaven dienen te worden ingezonden. De opgav
dient te bevatten: naam en voorletters van den belanghebbende, rang,
ambt of functie, woonplaats en leeftijd, alsmede tot welke categorie
(a of b, hieronder bedoeld) de persoon, met wie(n) de belanghebbende
gehuwd is, behoort.
Voor zooveel noodig merk ik nog op, dat ingevolge artikel 4 van de
Verordening No.189/1940 :
a. Jood is een ieder, die uit tenminste drie naar ras voljoodsche
   grootouders stamt, terwijl
b. als Jood wordt aangemerkt hij, die uit twee voljoodsche grootouders stamt en zelf op den negenden Mei 1940 tot de Joodsch-
   kerkelijke gemeente heeft behoord of na dien datum daarin wordt
   opgenomen"

Op grond van deze circulaire ziet het Bestuur zich derhalve belast
met het verzamelen van de in die circulaire bedoelde gegevens. Ik
verzoek U, indien U gehuwd bent met een persoon, die Jood(Jodin) is
of als Jood (Jodin) beschouwd moet worden, mij de verlangde gegevens
schriftelijk te verstrekken voor zover deze tenminste niet reeds in
het adresboekje van onze school vermeld staan. Van degenen, die mij
geen opgave inzenden, zal ik aannemen, dat zij niet gehuwd zijn met
een Jood (Jodin) of als Jood(Jodin) te beschouwen persoon, zodat ik
wat hen betreft met een negatieve opgave zal volstaan.

Voor toezending van de vereiste gegevens aan onderstaand adres vóór
Zaterdag 26 September 1942 houd ik mij aanbevolen.

Amsterdam, 23 September 1942

                              Th.Limperg
                              Secretaris

                              Heerengracht 455, Amsterdam

Another Nazi directive: memorandum to teachers at the
Amsterdam Lyceum directing them to declare marriage to a
Jewish spouse

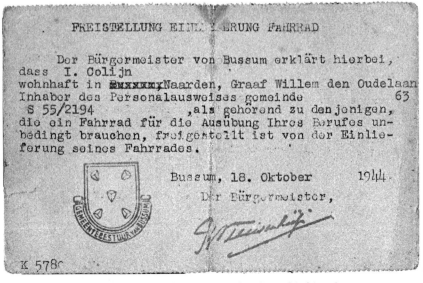

Dad gets a four-hour permit to gather wood.

A Nazi "favor"—Dad is permitted to keep his bicycle as a
necessary tool of trade.

When Ruin's Wheel Rolled O'er Us—Dad illustrates his memoirs.

PART THREE

What Have We Learned About Genocide?

What Have We Learned About Genocide?

Are there any lessons that derive from reading about the war through my father's eyes or reading and learning about the Holocaust through encounters with scholars and others met along the way?

It may be useful to sketch the main causes of genocide as I have come to understand them. Elie Wiesel believes that the Holocaust ultimately falls beyond comprehension, and some survivors I know hold to the view that no one can understand the Holocaust who was not part of it. One must respectfully disagree. Genocidal events are man-made, they have causes, they run their course, and they can be analyzed and explained. Such explanation may well lead to further questions because the quest for knowledge does not have a finish line. Moreover, as we have seen with the national reassessments about World War II, that quest is under frequent social reconstruction. Moreover, while that quest is on, new events take place. There have repeated instances of genocide since World War II: we have barely begun to analyze the last instance when the next genocide rolls in. It is like swimming against the surging surf. Every case expands the canvas for comparative analysis but there are some basic elements that can be described.

What *is genocide*? There is not a great deal of agreement on the definition of the term. Even if we dispense with obvious misapplications of the term for political intent, for example, when abortion is called genocide, there remains a great deal of disagreement about the meaning of the term. Scott Straus, in a seminal article in the *Journal of Genocide Research,* summarized some twenty definitions of the term just among leading genocide scholars, different among such vectors as genocidal intent, the formulation of such intent, the manner wherein genocide is carried out, the agents of such intent, and differentiation among targeted victims.

In the UN Convention on Genocide, *genocide* is defined as "acts committed with intent to destroy, in whole or in part, a national, ethnical, racial or religious group, as such." There are a number of problems with that definition. Intent is not always easy to prove and, if so, often too late. The definition excludes the mass murder of political opponents to a regime or a social class because the Soviet Union balked at such inclusion at the time. What is to be made of "in part"? How much killing is enough to establish that genocide is under way? What is to be made of the concepts of race and ethnicity? Not only is membership hard to define but the concept of race has no biological meaning. Straus, therefore, prefers the term "organic collectivity" which would include non-racial, non-ethnic political groupings.

In essence, genocidal victims belong to groups that, in the eyes of the perpetrating beholder, warrant to be targeted. That warrant, in turn, is based on ideology, a belief, for example, the belief in colonizers' superiority over indigenous populations or the revolutionary belief that society can be remade by genocide.

It is useful to turn to those beliefs, the notions of race, ethnicity, nationality, religion, and colonial or imperial expansion because these are the main causes of genocide as I have come to understand them. Thereafter, we will move to some possible areas of future inquiry and conclude with a few comments about the academic subculture of genocide studies today.

Violence

The keystone to understanding genocide is the human propensity toward violence. If it were not for that propensity, genocide would not exist: sometimes things are as simple as that. Let us, therefore, first focus on violence.

I am not a violent man, not now, but it was not always so. Student hazing, for example, was often wildly funny but occasionally violent as well, though there was never sexual violence: nobody got sodomized or sexually abused in anger. But hazing could be sadistic, even lethal. The captain of a Dutch men's field hockey team decided it was good fun to re-enact Wilhelm Tell and drive a meatball off a freshman's head with a hockey stick. He killed him. The apex of violence was the so-called "infighting." All freshmen from one student *corps*, still with their heads shaven, would head for another university *corps* building for a full scale assault, hundreds of your side trying to pour in, hundreds of defenders trying to keep you out, with water hoses, beer, rotten tomatoes, and eggs—and fists. I still have a nice scar from a broken beer glass used in anger, then a trophy palm, now an embarrassment. One day, we invaded the building of *Unitas*, the student *corps* at the *Vrije Universiteit*, fought our way in, took over the beer pumps, and threw a concert piano out of the window. Grand it was, Steinway grand. It startled the transvestites across the street, at *Madame Arthur*. Had Philip Glass been there and heard 88 strings broken up, he might have mused: "Goodness, I better score some silence."[15] I am not a violent man, not now. I have not hit anyone in anger, except verbally, since my student days. I have never beaten a woman, something of no particular distinction, of course. I do not own a gun, though doing so does not infer a propensity toward violence.

But I have, for a brief time, known the strange seduction of group violence, alcohol fueled, and the power of the purposeful, wilding collective, bonded by love of club and country (or ideology). Years later, I read Bill Buford's *Among the Thugs*, about the time he spent among soccer hooligans, and the mesmerizing tale of the overwhelming beauty he felt around him when a few hundred Manchester United fans terrorized the entire center of Turin after a match. Buford describes the simple exhilaration and beauty, the "nihilistic purity" when civilization is swept aside when a crowd commits an act of violence. I did not recoil in judgment but in recognition. It is the part scholars may well miss, toiling in their studies among their texts. Victims know—they know the end of the stick. I know the beginning of the stick because, for a brief time, I have seen the capacity that lurks in me. Hans Magnus Enzensberger got some of it right in his book *Civil Wars*, and the entire oeuvre of the Polish war journalist, Ryszard Kapuściński is a good guide to understanding.[16] So is the work of Ernst Jünger who revered the glory of war in *Storm of Steel*, before eventually coming to oppose Hitler, and much can be learned from the work of Georges Sorel.[17] Once you know the beast, even for brief moments, in an "unplugged" sense of self, you can begin the journey of constant restraint, and thank the gods that you have not been put in situations where those carefully nurtured restraints can snap. It does not take much: Milgram and Zimbardo showed that in experiments; I know this from experience.[18] The sudden, unexpected situation can be right around the bend. If such a situation occurs, let us hope that you are not there because you covet the transforming, adrenalin induced euphoria, the sheer happiness when things are "going to go off" as soccer hooligans say. The refusal to succumb to the siren of collective violence can be difficult, and those who have had a taste of it know how true that is. In the safe confines of academe, one easily overlooks this point. Bill Buford certainly knew: read his book!

Soccer or student violence is, of course, child's play compared to the largest canvas of violence: war, but there is a continuum. Elements of the exaltation of a violent environment, of its extraordinary (though dark) beauty, and of its mythologizing power are recognized by Chris Hedges, in his introduction of *War Is a Force That Gives Us Meaning*. Here, a seasoned war correspondent (with a master of divinity from Harvard University), sketches the "lethal addiction" of war. Hedges concludes that "war is a drug." Christopher Browning's study of quite ordinary men who were involved in the killing of Jews made clear that the tipping point to its addiction is pretty close, and that we easily slide from more or less normal moral behavior to immoral monstrosity. There is little to add to this but there is a broader culture wherein such addiction takes place, or is even encouraged.

Intoxicated students and soccer hooligans recognize the dark siren song of collective violence but that song can permeate an entire culture in a broad, systemic and modern canvas. William Pfaff argues in *The Bullet's Song: Romantic Violence and Utopia* that the roots of the collective violence in modern warfare must be laid at the doorstep of nineteenth century political romanticism. Individual chivalry gave way to the clarion call of new messiahs who saw society as perfectible only through the redemption of utopian violence. A string of romantic warriors passes through Pfaff's study: T.E. Lawrence (Lawrence of Arabia), Willi Münzenberg (the founder and master propagandist of the international communist movement *Komintern*), Gabriele D'Annunzio who established a proto-fascist statelet, Fiume, Ernst Jünger and André Malraux, who all believed in revolutionary utopias and the notion that the catharsis of violence was the only way to transform society but that the engaged struggle—with its blood, sweat, and sacrifice—was also the only way for man (sic) to prove himself (and to find confirmation, even pleasure, along the way). Millions are seduced by these siren songs though, in case we forget Gandhi altogether, it should be noted that utopias do not have to be based on collective violence as a prerequisite condition. However, among genocide scholars, we find similar notions on the interstices of wars and genocide.

Collective violence gives us purpose, may give us power, resolve, a "high" in the vernacular, and Hedges provides biting insights why collective violence holds such varied attractions over us. Of course, one must read about actual warfare, its carnage, its sadism, its sexual violence, and its victims to debunk the myths behind the reasons-of-the-day to go to war and to mitigate the notion of war-as-a-drug. Hedges, like other war correspondents before him, leaves little doubt that war remains hell. To borrow from one of the better television comedies of our time: war myth makers, curb your enthusiasm.

Racism

After violence and after those who turn a human frailty into a celebrated good, what other beliefs underpin genocide? In the Holocaust, the key to Nazi ideology is antisemitism, which found its expression in a pseudo-scientific cauldron of vitriol—the concept of race, with Germans at the top, other races on lower rungs, and Jews at the very bottom.

Let me briefly expand on the notion of race because racism is not unique to the Nazi ideology. The quest for control of new materials and other economic resources and its twin engine, the quest for control of export markets formed the economic imperative for colonialism and imperialism. Missionary zeal interlocked with this quest to give the quest religious cachet and justification. The differentiation of species in the natural world after the Darwinist revolution took us, in turn, to the emergence of race as a concept in Western thinking, as Ivan Hanaford argued in *Race: The History of an Idea in the West*. We know how the idea of race mutates into "scientific racism" wherein bad science transforms a few genetic or physiognomic differences into a scientifically unsupportable pecking order (read for starters Leon Poliakov, *The Aryan Myth*).

That pecking order has lethal consequences. It takes us from eugenics to euthanasia, to the Nuremberg laws and on to the Holocaust, but also to other genocides. The Rwandan genocide, for instance, is based on presumed differences between Hutu and Tutsi, clearly built as a social construct on scientific quicksand. Racism, then, needs to be explored not only because of the lethal effect to which it has been put in the extermination of minorities and the pseudo-scientific justification thereof, but also because the very concept of race has no sustainable scientific meaning whatsoever. We share 98 percent of our DNA with chimpanzees, and among the remaining 2 percent there is not a hell of a lot to differentiate the human species in support of the notion that one group of DNA shareholders is better than another group with an ever so slightly different portfolio.

In brief, the appearance of race at the core of Nazi ideology, for example, is not just a culmination of centuries-long antisemitism, but finds its genesis in the late arrival of the idea of race in the West. There is an explanation for that late arrival but no scientific base for the idea itself.

Nationalism

Like racism, the idea of the nation-state is a relatively new phenomenon in human history. If we measure human existence in millions of years, the concept of sovereign nation-states has been around for just the briefest part. It emerged in 1648 with the Peace of Westphalia that concluded a thirty-year war in Europe, carved up the Hapsburg Empire a bit, and gave birth, for example, to the independent Dutch Republic. Prior to that, mankind had been organized in roaming and hunting families, clans, tribes, feudal fiefs, city-states or empires of various cohesion but the sense of nationhood proved to be a powerful way to organize humans in yet a new structure, the sovereign nation-state. Based sometimes on ethnicity or on economic ties, sometimes on language or culture, often on shared common history and experience, a sense of nationhood answers the human "need of belonging" as Freud put it a long time ago in *Group Psychology and the Analysis of the Ego*. Belonging to a group or culture, to a collective identity, gives us comfort. However, nationalism is, of course, a micro-political concept: nationalism means "us" vs. "them," and the others are different from us.

Especially after the French Revolution when ideas of freedom, liberty, and equality emerge and join with the notion that the nation-state is the most apt political framework to establish these ideas, it becomes clear that nationalism is at the apex of influential "isms" in the past few centuries: under the democratic pulse that runs through the nineteenth century, nationalism becomes a code word for mass political participation and emancipation. The desire for egalitarianism and democracy made modern nationalism a powerful idea indeed.

Of course, there are drawbacks. Like racism, the internal unifying strength of nationalism is inherently centrifugal to the global system. Strong nationalism often triggers xenophobia, the institutionalization of large standing armies (feudal lords could only engage in limited conflict, with hired mercenaries), the persecution of minorities not deemed as belonging to the nation, for example, Germany's Jews, or the annihilation of indigenous populations who stand in the way of a nation-state's full blooming, as happened in the Americas. Inherent in nationalism is the self-satisfied belief in one state's superiority, which may lead to imperial ambition: think of the so-called "white man's burden" and the Nazi desire to create *Lebensraum* (living space) for the so-called Aryan race.

When a nation-state's political culture believes that it is the best political arrangement in the world, such a culture contributes to internal legitimacy but it also serves to extend influence elsewhere. Ronald Reagan's core belief, shared with other US presidents, was that the United States is a "city upon the hill," mankind's last best hope.[19] That idea underpinned the Reagan administration's foreign policy behavior, for example, the shift from the Cold War notion of containment of communism to one aimed to roll communism back. Such ambitions may unify a people at home, thus becoming a source of power in and by itself, but also establish international objectives. Reagan saw rolling back communism as the best way to protect the "American way of life," as some see the war on terrorism today. Thus, nationalism is a cause and a means of international behavior but its ambitions become geopolitical ends. That combination makes nationalism a very powerful force in international relations, as well as a strong factor within the nation-state. The sense of nationhood gives meaning to our past, shapes our present and future, and, in democratic society, helps maintain society by consent rather than coercion. Thus, nationalism is a powerful tool not only for tyrants with international ambitions but also for democratic political elites: both can use nationalism to give legitimacy to their international ambitions as people rally around the flag, a cause, or a leader. A country's economic system finds internal legitimacy in nationalism as well, witness the old saying "What is good for GM is good for America."

Nationalism means cognitive consonance, a necessary glue to keep a country together, but it may also lead to periods with chilling impact on democratic dissonance, such as during the McCarthy era in the Cold War or the "love it or leave it" cry against opponents of the Vietnam war. Dissent, of course, may well be an act of noble patriotism but when a society is in international conflict, much of public opinion will not see it that way. And when the state becomes a semi-immortal God, requiring fanatic emotional attachment of its citizens, and when parochial love of country rises to a fever pitch in its hatred of others, the drums of war or the slaughters of genocide are often not far behind.

Aggressive nationalist projection overseas also puts severe stress on the American constitutional system, and not just in terms of civil liberties. In that domain, the left and, across the aisle, libertarians share a presumptive interest in protecting individuals against their governments, though libertarians have a stronger historical pedigree of concern: many on the left too often stand ready to abandon liberties when it serves their purpose. The more complex, more subtle objection to aggressive international ambition comes from conservatives who see the dangers to the American constitutional system in an institutional sense. Scholars such as Andrew J. Bacevich (*The New American Militarism*) and Ivan Eland (*The Empire Has No Clothes: US Foreign Policy Exposed*), rail against a militarist Leviathan that puts the country's economy on a permanent war footing completely at odds with the intent of the framers of the constitution. Such projection torques the checks and balance system strongly toward the executive branch, with a supine Congress and a US Supreme Court unwilling to enforce the right of Congress to declare war, for example. Such projection also allows, even in the post-Cold war era, the continuing existence of a military-industrial complex—something Eisenhower warned against in his farewell address.

As a result of the Nazi era with its exalted idea of the German nation and Hitler's perceived necessity to kill Germany's main enemy, the Jews, and as a result of Stalinism and a Communist regime that destroyed yet other millions with totalitarian efficiency, and as a result of the incessant quarrels in the nation-state system throughout the first half of the twentieth century, many statesmen and scholars became interested in different ways to organize mankind after World War II. Such interest brought attempts to make the United Nations stronger than its predecessor, the establishment of intergovernmental organizations such as the IMF and World Bank, and the concept of a transnational Europe. There are several paths to do such undertakings, for example, the so-called routes of functionalism and neo-functionalism, which aim to bring about more social and economic cooperation in the hope that there will be political spill-over effects, hence fewer conflicts and war, or federalism, a primarily political route. All aimed at larger communities of consent than the divisive nation-state system. Thus, the post-war period with its expansion of international and transnational (or supranational) arrangements was a period of some hope that there could be less enmity, less "us" vs. "them," despite the Cold War that also had us in its grips.

However, the communitarian ambitions in Europe have not replaced centuries of separate nationalisms. Few among those loosely labeled "liberal internationalists" foresaw the breakup of the Soviet Union and the rise of ethno-nationalism to which it would give birth. Moreover, we still deal with the ambitions of nations that have not succeeded in their ambition of statehood, for example, the Basques in Spain or the Tamils in Sri Lanka, or we face nations that feel they have not succeeded in their national political ambitions, as happened after the breakup of Yugoslavia. In many places this results in terror, such as in the Caucasus, or in genocide as in the Balkans. Sobered by recent history, it is clear that nationalism remains a strong, powerful, often destructive force.

However, there are glimmers of hope. In several, particularly smaller states, the more dangerous facets of nationalism are weakening because their political cultures themselves are becoming less nationalist, perhaps even post-nationalist. Internally, that may create problems of governance but in the global system, there are distinct advantages: it is almost inconceivable that a weakly nationalist state such as Belgium could entertain genocidal ambitions. Of course, post-nationalism goes only so far. There is a balancing act in play. If a state becomes ungovernable, a "failed state" in the current parlance, then the conditions for genocide may be as ripe as under the fanatic nationalism of the Nazis.

Religion

In addition to racism and nationalism, genocide is often the result of religious beliefs though today's fundamentalism is only one form of a problem that has vexed mankind for many centuries.

In the face of carnage, Dostoevsky's Ivan Karamazov questions, "What claim can the creator of a harmony, of which all this is a part, have to be a moral authority?"[20] Right on, Ivan. I don't know what to make of God in the face of Auschwitz though I stand in awe of survivors who did not lose their faith. Some even find ontological answers in their experience. My colleague Murray Kohn, for example, a child survivor of Auschwitz (where he spent years) not only is a rabbi of strong faith but, against the backdrop of the Holocaust, writes with passion in defense of God.

It is not up to us to sit in judgment, no matter how incomprehensible such faith strikes us. But we are a post-war generation that is very secularized, which underwent "deconfessionalization" and left the church in droves. Many of us are uncertain agnostics, and the very act of such self-identification makes us sometimes uncomfortable: is doing so blasphemous? We find our moral compass not in church, synagogue, or mosque but in aspects of humanism, liberalism, socialism, Buddhism, and, yes, in "Christian precepts"—concern for the poor, for instance—or in the writings of theologians such as Reinhold Niebuhr who understood that the road to hell could be paved with the moral aspirations and good intentions of Christianity *per se*. Tidy it is not: our search is constant, it evolves, and it is never over but by and large we manage to coalesce on some core principles, though true believers critique our post-modern relativism. In our complex journey we are sometimes reminded of a witticism of Groucho Marx: "These are my principles. If you don't like them, I have others."

However, the absence of a hermetically sealed worldview does not mean we don't give shape to principled contours in our thoughts as the journey moves on. For instance, we may not be sure about God but we do have pretty clear views on organized religion. In my case the dour vicar of the Dutch Reformed Church had nothing to offer my shattered mother when my dad died at 56 but the question whether he had been ready to die. At 56? "You must be joking," as John McEnroe used to say. At the time, I was preparing for Confirmation which happens when you reach eighteen (Sunday school was on Wednesday night). I dropped out, with my mother's permission: a Church unwilling or incapable of providing comfort was of no use to me. We were studying the Moabites at the time. The Old Testament held little charm: too much genocidal carnage, frankly.

Dutch society was built on religious pillars that segmented society in ways that make you understand that apartheid was a Dutch concept, borne out of the notion of the nineteenth century Protestant leader Abraham Kuyper, who believed in the sovereignty of each religious grouping in its own substratum. There were religious political parties, Catholic, of course, but no less than three Protestant ones as well; Catholic and various Protestant radio and television stations, schools, sport leagues. Add to that the segmentation of secular parties, newspapers from communist to liberal (read: conservative, in the continental context) and it was, as Arend Lijphart describes in *The Politics of Accomodation*, only a *modus vivendi* among the political elites that kept the country from complete dysfunctionality. The post-war generation had little patience for this fragmentation, and certainly for the notions that God was with us, only with our church; that only our brand of religion is right; or that those who disagree will go to hell.

We knew about different hells. During the independence war of the Dutch against the Hapsburg Empire, an eighty year Protestant-Catholic struggle (that started in 1568 and would end in the Peace of Westphalia in 1648), the Spanish had encircled the doubly-moated fortress city of Naarden, my hometown. The year was 1572. The starving (and freezing) inhabitants eventually surrendered when the Spanish promised no retributions after the siege. They then forced everyone into an orphanage and killed every single man, woman, and child. For good order, they also burned the city down. The people of Naarden had paid with their lives for the meaning of the Catholic notion *Nulla salus extra ecclesium:* outside the Church there is no salvation. Religious wars and their consequences we understood. We knew about the Crusades and how that *Nulla* notion had led to the massacre of the Albigensians in the thirteenth century under the papacy of Pope Innocent (sic) III. We knew about the Inquisition. Naarden's destruction was part of the story. Later, my paternal ancestors would flee France. They were Huguenots (in case there are ever reparations one would hope the Colijns get a nice castle back).

There is an odd logic to the concept of *Nulla*. *My* faith is the only judge of human action and the meaning of life. If there is salvation out-side of my faith, then the previous sentence cannot be true. So, who is right? Biblical sectarianism is brilliantly spoofed in Monty Python's *The Life of Brian*. Free of the sardonic fun poked at sectarianism in the film, but equally poignant, is the poetic tale once told by the Iranian film maker Mohsen Makhmalbaf. Truth is really a mirror that broke when it fell from the hand of God. Everyone picked up a piece of it, and each decided that the truth was what they saw reflected in their fragment rather than realizing that truth had become fragmented among them all.

It is a truism that religious faith, especially in its fundamentalist man-ifestations, is often exclusionary. History is replete with religious mas-sacres that show that religious fervor frequently entails the death of oth-ers, the unbelievers: millions have been sacrificed on its altar. Americans can read all about it in the easily accessible work of Karen Armstrong, for example, *The Battle for God* or *Holy War: The Crusades and Their Impact on Today's World*. Beginning with the internecine murder and unspeakable brutality that riddles the Old Testament, every monotheistic religion seems to have long periods of savage gestation: stone the aldulteress, smite the infidel, sometimes stoned on hashish as the Shi'ite *Hashishim* were before going on their missions against religious enemies (the origin of the term *assassin*). In the face of the post 9/11 obsession with Wahhabism, it is useful to remember the nearly universal violence of centuries of religious "molting," as my friend Yair Cohen calls it. It is not limited to Abrahamic faiths: In Japanese musea you can see the halberds of Buddhist monks, their favorite weapon, three yards long.

Of course, like you, I know many pious Christians, Jews, Muslims, Quakers, Baha'is and those of other faiths who do nothing but good in direct consequence of their faith. I read Teilhard de Chardin and I am floored (and not only because it is hard to read in French). I am deeply moved by the beauty of Bach's "Jesu, Joy of my Desiring," and his *Matthew Passion* grabs me by the throat each Easter, even knowing to what abuse of Jews it has been put in the history of its performances at Oberammergau, and not knowing whether Jesus was the son of God, though He certainly thought so. I am envious of the faithful with their deep sense of belonging.

But I also know this: those who do not share our fragment of the mirror, Roma, Sinti, Armenians, Jews, Ibos, Kampucheans, Hindus, Muslims, are tragically often washed away by the victimizer on the altar of his God—garbage, as Ivan Klíma writes in *Love and Garbage.* The Apocalypse, in Klíma's words, is "increasingly becoming a mere technical problem." I, for one, was not surprised by the vitriolic text of Osama bin Laden's declaration of war upon the West a few years ago. Here we find combined the true believer's credo that there is no path but the path of Allah, with the political ambition, borrowed from Sayyid Qutb, the founder of modern Islamic fundamentalism, to establish a pan-Islamic empire, a new caliphate. Al Qaeda's political-religious utopia brought us 9/11. Paul Williams suggests in *The Al Queda Connection* that sleeper cells and nuclear devices may be pre-positioned in the United States. The possibility that Islamo-terrorists may require weapons of mass destruction is the subject of great concern in the intelligence communities and among people in several countries. Is it any wonder that religious utopias scare the bejeezus out of us? The dark side of the religious moon has always concerned me. I don't seem to find the flexibility of Groucho Marx to change *that* particular view.

Totalitarianism

The dangers do not simply rest in our individual propensity toward violence, in the joys of collective violence, in racism, in nationalism, or in the fervor of religious fanaticism of every stripe. Earlier, reference was made to those who romanticize violence as a way to transform society. The transformative idea lodges in virtually all-encompassing ideological worldviews. In the secular world, the concept of the perfectibility of the human condition is a direct consequence of the Enlightenment, and intellectuals are especially susceptible to this idea. Intellectuals, as Michael Howard, François Furet, Jean-François Revel, Václav Havel, and many others have pointed out, believe to be the only ones who understand the forces of history and how those forces can be altered to change society: reasoning men can control its direction. Intellectuals think that they know everything better. Therefore, they insist on the authority to improve the world according to their vision. Our world can be improved by human effort, made "wonderful," as Yaacov Talmon wrote in his warning, *The Origins of Totalitarian Democracy,* by values "for all of humanity"—values that replace the state's limits on human freedom, secular values that replace religion. The attraction of closed reasoning and all-inclusive abstractions are of particular interest to intellectuals whose sense of intelligent superiority leads them to the belief they can improve on the imperfections of democracy, of the exercise of individual rights and freedom, and of market economies.

Sweep it all away. To the loneliness of true intellectuals, the party, the proletariat, the Führer, forced change through (perpetual) war, and the attainment of power are all concepts that provide a sense of belonging, of protection, and, most of all, they are pathways through which they can control the world: intentions justify all means, and if the weak, the other, the non-believer needs to be swept away too during the march to salvation inherent in the new worldview, so be it. Thus, Pol Pot, the Sorbonne educated honcho of the Cambodian genocide could say that he had a clear conscience. Thus, many on the left refused to face the horrific realities of Stalin and Mao, and those on the right refused to see the lethal dangers of fascism, or made their careers by embracing and implementing its goals—witness the highly educated group of men who planned "the final solution" at Wannsee. When the notion emerges in the body politic that there is but one truth, we are on the dangerous, anti-liberal road of "political messianism" as Talmon phrased it—Robespierre, Marx, Trotsky, Mao, Stalin, Hitler. In that sense, classic liberalism is the only viable option because it inherently rejects the notion that there is but one political truth.

In the face of atrocity that wiped out yet another civilization in Turkey there is a saying *Dur Yolcu bilmeden Gelip basttgin bu toprak bir devrin battiği verdir,* Hail, wayfarer; the land over which your feet has been treading so lightly has seen the fall of an era. Musa Dagh, Sobibor, Babi Yar, Belzec.[21] The steps go on. Political terrorism has drawn its inspiration from the writings of Sartre, Marcuse, Hegel, and Marx. Secular utopias and its adherents, enthralled with the power of inflicting suffering and death upon millions who stand in the way of the Communist or Fascist masses en route to the Promised Land, can be every inch as lethal as religious utopias, especially in the hands of totalitarian, powerful, and determined governments. Among our predatory species, beware, especially, of universalizing intellectuals. In their tireless toiling for the "good of the whole," they often are the most carnivorous handmaidens of all. We say that the road to hell is paved with good intentions but it is really the other way around: the way to good intentions is paved with hell.

Some suggestions for the future

Now that we have some understanding of the causes of genocide, are there some lessons we can impart to those who study the Holocaust or genocide generally? In no particular order, I would like to focus on a few notions that may have some meaning for ourselves and for our children, for example, the treatment of others, style in our work, the need for some courage, the careful use of language, the necessity to study other languages, honesty with our own national narratives, and the problem with empathy, before reaching the conclusion of this part and this book.

Others

Henry Louis "Skip" Gates notes in *Loose Cannons: Notes on the Culture Wars* that there is something to be learned from Edward Said who once suggested that in the academy we should be migrants, traveling among other selves, other identities so that the academy can transform conflicting assertions into the kind of creative interaction that might lead to reconciliation, mutuality, and recognition. Dan Bar-On's work certainly tries to do that.

Yehuda Bauer, in a farewell ditty to us when he and his wife Elana returned to Jerusalem, mused that "All in all, it is nice that we are Jews" but also suggested with typical good humor:

> But equally how nice it is to love all human faces
> Black and white, and brown and yellow, of all races
> To feel at one with Russians, Hindu and Chinese
> And even the Lubavitcher, if you please.[22]

It is not always so. In fact, it is rarely so. The parochial self-referential and self-indulgent life of academicians has been spoofed mercilessly by the likes of Jane Smiley and David Lodge. Campuses are full of such self-indulgence. We bury ourselves in our specialties and, to the extent that they are "victim studies" as their detractors often call them, there is generally little attention for the other, on the contrary: the calamities we study are in competition as is still the case to some degree in genocide work. I wrote earlier that there cannot be a pyramid of suffering. It is worth repeating. Also, as we look at the world through the particularist prism of ethnicity and—given the carnage that results from ethnic conflict—one often does, there are two important points to be made.

Competition across calamities creates hegemony in memory, runs counter to Said, and constitutes a crisis of substance. Perhaps many of us are simply too smug in our own victimhood, too comfortable in our own cognitive and ethnic milieu to make a genuine effort to travel among other selves. It is, again, necessary to underscore that ethnicity and race are often confused but that the concept of race is a social construct. Some students may come from backgrounds where racism, casual or not, is a quite common part of social intercourse. In scientific terms race is a rather meaningless concept: students should know why. However, we don't help them do that if we engage in partisan, ethnic polemics.

Style

Oscar Wilde once contended: "style is everything, substance but a passing myth." A few words on style are in order. In his memoirs, *The Story of a Life,* Aharon Appelfeld laments some of the disputes that arose, over time, among survivors who began to gather at The New Life Club in Tel Aviv in 1950. Appelfeld concludes that terrible catastrophes don't change human weaknesses, but entrench old habits, from conceit to deceit. There are few areas of study that raise the same passions as Holocaust and genocide studies. That is understandable enough but less defensible is the disappearance of elementary manners. I have heard scholars accuse other scholars of engagement in Nazi practices. I have heard scholars refer to a colleague they disagree with as a fraud, or a racist, or even that old stand-by, "motherfucker." Such epithets contribute remarkably little to the advancement of scientific discourse.

Conceit deserves special mention. Australians refer to the "tall poppy syndrome" when they encounter self-important blowhards.[23] The conference circuits, including the Holocaust circuit, are full of them, jockeying for prime time slots, carrying on well beyond their allotted panel time at the expense of others, the self-aggrandizing hawkers of scholarly "breakthroughs," who believe their own or their publisher's press releases. Given the subject matter, they are vile. One would expect less puffery. It often does not work that way although the real stars in my field sometimes are surprisingly modest and self-effacing, my dear colleague Carol Rittner, for instance, or her regular co-author John K. Roth. There is decorum in industry with modesty. Blowhards might take note that, even when he is giving a lecture, Elie

Wiesel is typically the quietest person in a room. Mind you, I see no problem with prima donnas in Physics or in Art History, and certainly not on the soccer pitch. We all understand, in V.S. Pritchett's memorable words, "our need for modest swellings of self-esteem, our greed for plump little vanities." But the subject matter of genocide studies requires demeanor more respectful of the dead. There is considerable irony in bad behavior among academics. During some twenty years of interaction with students learning about genocide I have never encountered any of the nonsense I have just described. Students are invariably respectful, serious. They leave their egos at home when they are confronting genocidal history. We can learn from them.

Language

There is a different element of style in the use of language in genocide study. Here are just a few to ponder. Whichever genocide we commemorate, let's do so without the exhortation "Lest we forget." Please! "Lest we forget—lest we forget!" is the last line of every verse in Kipling's "Recessional," his musings on the ascendance of the British Empire at the time of Queen Victoria's Jubilee. White Man's Burden Kipling was, of course, no stranger to the notion of British racial superiority and, as Harry Ricketts notes in his biography *Rudyard Kipling—A Life,* the poem endorsed the rightfulness of the "Dominion over palm and pine" or the control over the "lesser breeds" in the empire. Later in life, Kipling would pen some nasty antisemitic poems.[24] After World War I he was susceptible to Jewish world conspiracy theories: we do better to remember without this wholly inappropriate phrase.

Others have commented on the inappropriate notion that Auschwitz and the other camps were "liberated." The allies stumbled upon them. Equally irritating is the appropriation of the Holocaust for other social issues, from environmental degradation to abortion. It demeans the former and adds little but confusion to the issues at hand. In brief, a little care with language is a good idea.

Wrangling over language often centers on the definition of *genocide* and its meaning in international law. There are quite serious implications, such as the obligation to intervene, when the UN definition of *genocide* is met. These are far from easy matters. However, Samantha Power eloquently indicts such wrangling in *A Problem from Hell* (see note 11). Great and small powers often fiddle with definitional issues to the point that a genocidal event nears its conclusion before anyone acts. Unlike the earlier cases, where language use is sloppy, here it is the attention to precision that creates the problem: definitional hair splitting often masquerades a lethal absence of political will.

Other languages

A few years ago I met a French woman, Christine Loreau who works at *Civisme et Democracie* (Civitas and Democracy). She had with her a document with a call to action from the early days of the genocide in Rwanda, ten Hutu commandments cast in a vitriol that had an uncanny resemblance to the Nazi propaganda of Julius Streicher against the Jews.[25] Virtually no American undergraduate and few graduate students are able to read this French text, never mind comparing it with its German antecedents, and yet such ability is critical to the analysis of the pre-genocidal phase in Rwanda, and elsewhere. It has been a few decades since the late Paul Simon (D-Ill.) described language deficiencies among Americans as a scandal but little has changed. In a 2003 study of the American Council on Education, one percent of Americans are studying Arabic, two percent Chinese. The national security implications of facing the world blind, deaf, and dumb are obvious, from intelligence gathering to fighting wars. The implications for genocide studies are equally serious. Those in the English speaking world who want to study, for example, the reassessment of the war and the Holocaust in The Netherlands, are dependent on a few English sources, such as Bob Moore's *Victims and Survivors: The Nazi Persecution of the Jews in the Netherlands.* It is a good book but English-only scholars cannot verify its assertions. Language problems cause epistemological insularity and flaws: any analysis is unlikely to be complete unless texts that give witness to genocide can be understood.

Pluck

There may, on occasion, be the need for some courage in one's work.

In general, and within the context of the bureaucracy of academe, I have always been an adherent to Burke's political philosophy that representatives (in my world, chairs and deans) owe those they represent not only their industry but also their opinion. You ought not to sacrifice your views to the prevailing winds of popular opinion. Equally, we should not "roll" in anticipatory reaction when calculations predict that the provost or president may not agree with us. Academic leaders are paid to think, not to be sycophants or cheerleaders. Thinking may not always help your career (it may advance differently if you decide to shut up) but being a courtier is not an honorable existence: kicking down and kissing up seldom is. You need to look at yourself in the mirror each day. Also, open architecture of opinion is usually better for the institutions we serve. It is probably much the same in corporate management.

Sometimes we encounter situations that require a bit of physical pluck. In the mid-1970s I visited *La Colonio Tovar,* a very authentic German Black Forest village in the high mountains of Venezuela. At dinner in a restaurant, a few drinking louts broke out in the *Horst Wessel* song, the top stand-by of Nazis and neo-Nazis alike. I threw over our table and its food, startled the merry makers by shouting in German I did not care for this shit, and stomped out. Frankly, I was pretty scared they would follow me but it was the right thing to do.

In the mid-1990s I chaired the US Committee of a large Holocaust conference in Berlin. The conference leadership had received some nasty threats from neo-Nazis. Several members of the US Committee opted out. I borrowed a bullet-proof vest from the campus police: better safe than sorry. Sarah, our young daughter, and I had to change planes at Heathrow. As we were landing, the plane suddenly veered away. The pilot told us the runway was under mortar attack by the IRA. Our hearts were in our throats. After we got to the gate, a young English mom near us crisply got up and told her brood, "Chip, chip, get a wiggle on." Pluck! In Berlin, I took the vest off once, in Berlin's Turkish section. I figured neo-Nazis would not go to a Turkish restaurant. There was not much pluck here, besides just going to Berlin when I was quite apprehensive. Courage is not about having no fear but being scared and then doing the right thing all the same. When confronting racism that is a good thing to remember.

Self-righteousness

We have come to see that the post-war generation tried to lift the "veil of positive national narrative," as my colleague Michael Hayse puts it. We gravitated toward those who share our critical views, such as the film makers Alain Resnais in the 1955 movie *Night and Fog* and Marcel

Ophuls whose critical view on France, *The Sorrow and the Pity,* we watched and watched again. We most certainly read John Hershey's *Hiroshima,* and perhaps more recently we read about Poland in *Neighbors* by Jan Gross. Many of us with ties to victims (or victims themselves) wrote out of anger, typified by Daniel Goldhagen's *Hitler's Willing Executioners* and those with ties to perpetrators write on the sense of parental betrayal they feel, and write for redemption. In this context, recall Gottfried Wagner's book. Generalizations about a generation take us only so far. They are vignettes. Michael Hayse reminded me that each attack on that positive national narrative, for example, a German critical exhibit, staged some years ago, on the role of the *Wehrmacht* in the "final solution," brings a popular backlash. Is there perhaps a limit on how much revisionism popular culture can digest, or has the role of public intellectuals been reduced so much that they no longer have a bearing on popular perception? Hayse also suggested that chronological distance, the benefit of hindsight, and more complete, big picture information than wartime leaders had at the time, may tend to simplify the complexities of decisions made in war. However, he also agrees that the third generation, our students—and certainly German students—are remarkably free of our weight. Youth tends to divide good and evil easily, but this generation may be more capable of seeing the war in more complex frames than we once did.

In the meantime, the second generation ages: our youthful armchair moralism wanes. Our disdain for perpetrators and bystanders becomes more measured because we have learned the ambiguities of wartime situations, especially those where people hold virtually absolute power over others. We have read our Remarque and Céline about war per se and may have read *Ethics and Air Power in World War II* by Stephen A. Garrett. My good/bad division bell began to shatter under the influence (again) of Harry Mulisch in his 1959 book *Het Stenen Bruidsbed* (*The Stone Bridal Bed* in the English version) about Dresden: "good" and "bad/*fout*/evil" was not the most useful prism to look through after all. Others learned the same lesson from Kurt Vonnegut's *Slaughterhouse Five.* We learned from the landmark experiments of Stanley Milgram on situational obedience, and we learned from Philip Zimbardo's Stanford Prison Experiment (see note 18) and, much later, Christopher Browning's *Ordinary Men: Reserve Police Battalion 101 and the Final Solution in Poland.* We benefit from Arthur G. Miller who edited *The Social Psychology of Good and Evil,* and from Thomas Blass who edited *Obedience to Authority: Current Perspectives on the Milgram Paradigm.* We know the gradual degradation of the moral compass among ordinary people in extraordinary circumstances. Guantanamo Bay and Abu Ghraib may disgust us but prison abuse can no longer surprise us. The derisive finger pointing of our youth has given way or should give way to sober reflection on the possibilities within us in extreme circumstances: "there, but for the grace of" and so on. We have come of age.

Isms

Earlier, we dealt with racism, nationalism, religious fanaticism, and totalitarianism. It is particularly the latter that has received attention because much work on genocide focuses on the twin scourges we fought in the twentieth century, Nazism and communism, and too little attention has been given to the consequences of our own imperial histories. There has been a change in the past decade. Mike Davis, in *Late Victorian Holocausts,* described the carnage resulting from colonial expansion during the nineteenth century; Adam Hochschild dealt with Belgium's Congo history in *King Leopold's Ghost,* and Ward Churchill turned to the Americas in *A Little Matter of Genocide.* If we are to be historically honest and morally relevant, genocide studies needs to reckon with the consequences of empire, colonialism, and neo-liberalism, especially given the current global ambitions of *hyperpower* America. We cannot disengage from the discussions about empire that began as long ago as Hobson, Schumpeter, and Marx and then waned in the triumphalism of neo-liberalism at the end of the last century.

As long as our own experiences with genocide, slavery, and racism remain at the margins, we evade the question, as Peter Novick put it, of what we have done to others. In the American case, popular culture and, to a degree, genocide studies remains remarkably unreflective of America's past: it constitutes an epistemological and moral blind spot that stains the field, reduces its moral influence and diminishes the social relevance. "What," as the cover of Peter Novick's study asks, "are we to make of the fact that while Americans spend millions of dollars recording a European crime, there is no museum of American slavery?" Confronting American omission, indifference, and the absence of political will in the face of genocide abroad was the subject of Samantha

Power in *A Problem from Hell* (see note 11). The possible future consequences of the fundamental direction of America's global policies must,
much more than hitherto, become the problem confronted at home. The
American experience, of course, is not the only one that needs attention.
Other countries need to focus on an honest reckoning with their histories, too, and that matter goes well beyond World War II.

Caring

To pay attention to the basis of genocide in empire, in colonialism,
or in geopolitical ambition means serious study of structural violence.
Much genocide takes place under conditions of war, not in isolation.
Therefore, we need to think with our heads, not just our hearts, about
the complexities that give rise to genocide and try to prevent its occur-
rence, and not just wring our hands when it happens yet again.
Attention to the recent genocide in Darfur dissipated when the tsuna-
mi struck in South-East Asia. Hurricane Katrina may well have the
same effect on both. We care but briefly. Much outpourings of shallow
public empathy is more about feeling good than doing good. Peter
West rejects such sentiments as "phony, ephemeral and cynical." Our
"ostentatious" caring simply shows others that we have empathy but the
compassion culture has little lasting effect: it is entirely unclear that
such sentimentality will lead students to acquire the instrumental skills
necessary to be actively engaged in the direction of a nation's foreign
policies or in genocide prevention.

There is no evidence yet that even the most responsible efforts to
sensitize students to genocidal atrocities and oppression have any effect.
Novick, for one, believes that attention to the Holocaust may desensi-
tize students to genocidal crimes of lesser scope. Of course, we have,
like Sisyphus, little choice but to keep trying but we clearly need to
assess the effectiveness of what we do in genocide education: we don't
know yet, with any degree of validity, what "works" and we have yet to
decide what that means.

Coda

My friend Yair Cohen (the Polish Jew in my Philadelphia story) is
among my most brilliant mates (his mother escaped from Janówska, a
labor and extermination camp near Lvov, four days before the violent
liquidation of the camp, aided by a guard who told her to run, and then

shot over her head—a "good" or "bad" German? Yair's father was a partisan in the woods). Yair grew up in Poland, Switzerland, Italy (briefly: he ran away from home when his parents decided on Israel), and Israel before I met him in Philadelphia. He went to film school at USC and eventually married an equally brilliant Japanese woman, Kasumi. Yair is deeply versed in Western thought and literature (he introduced me to Umberto Eco before most people had heard of him) and equally versed in Eastern philosophy and religion. One day, on a bench in a national park near San Francisco, he asked me: "So, what is the essence of what you do?" I managed a Sisyphean platitude about trying to move our mud ball a little higher upon the hill. "Ah, *Tikkun Olam* (healing the world), do you understand the arrogance in believing you can change it?" Well now, there was a thought. But with my belief about linear human progress long gone, it struck a chord.

The academic world is full of world improvers. The cheapest currency in academe consists of many coins of opinion on how to do just that. We often load our advice upon our students, even unsolicited, because we claim experience and because we know best, we think, what is good for them. Of course, often we are right. We don't envelop ourselves in the liberal arts without finding some nuggets of perennial value. Starting with Plato, and moving right along, we can certainly provide a useful landscape of thought and cognition to help shape minds, perhaps even lives, yet even the most well-intended advice can have horrifying consequences.

In the seventies and early eighties, I ran my college's overseas study program and recruited students quite actively. What better than a semester abroad for students nestled in the quiet confines of the Southern Jersey Pine Barrens, students who rarely ventured out of state, perhaps never out of the country, yet students whose understanding of different cultures, of languages, and of the global environment would help determine America's future, as citizens, some as leaders, in an increasingly interdependent world? Then three students died in a fiery road accident in Australia and another student, Tom, already a good friend, was in a second accident. He is in a wheelchair now yet became a doctor. These were the worst days in college history. *Tikkun Olam?* Hmm. Consequently, I have become weary about giving advice. My personality tends to be pro-active but one comes to know that one cannot foresee any future consequences of good intentions, even if the means to get there are fully legitimate and reasonable. It is sobering, but it cannot stop us from trying altogether either.

We should at minimum be mindful of the structural violence in most of the world, where the inattention of the rich condemns millions and millions to death by dearth of food, affordable medicine, safe drinking water. We should be mindful to our dearth of will to stop the thugs who ruin them, Pol Pot, Verwoerd, Pinochet, Marcos, Idi Amin, Mugabe, Mobutu.[26] Others would, of course, add Western leaders to this gallery of rogues (Indonesians have a case to add Hendrik Colijn to the list of leaders who committed atrocities upon them). Suggesting global remedies would take us well beyond the scope of this book in that one would have to examine current contending theories of International Relations and verify empirically the validity of the remedies proposed. Similarly, there is the issue of genocide prevention, the most critical question in the field but also one that falls beyond the scope of this narrative (I have written about it elsewhere). Here the purpose has simply been to derive a few lessons from a personal journey, an exercise that is now coming to conclusion.

Thinking people owe fidelity to their selves, what Levinas calls *constance à soi*, in their responsibility to others beyond just post-modern irony and contingency, and for me that means that we should study structures and processes that center around the vexing problems of class, inequality, oppression, brutality, war, and genocide. Such study requires deep, data based probing, serious work, not just cultural narrative, and being mindful we live in an age where competing epistemological narratives (c.f. intelligent design), in their clamor for equal validity, reduce truth to relativism or irrelevance as Jeremy Campbell argues in *The Liar's Tale: A History of Falsehood*.

Active engagement with contemporary society and history may leave us with more questions than answers. My colleague Carol Rittner, Elie Wiesel, and others repeatedly point this out in their work. But one may hope, when it is all said and done, to have made some positive difference. "It is," as Former British Foreign Secretary Sir Geoffrey Howe concludes in his political memoir, "something to be able to believe that the stone is a little higher up the hill than when we started." That is not much, there is no grand vision here, and it may be a modest hope. However, for most of us such hope is, in and by itself, sufficient to examine the world and to give meaning to our life based on what we find (rather than having truth revealed metaphysically), and, in so doing, craft a modicum of useful change.

Our Holocaust Resource Center has a simple lesson (Yehuda Bauer's) when our staff is on the road, teaching about the Holocaust to young school children: don't be a perpetrator, don't be a victim, and don't be a bystander.

In W.H. Auden's wonderful poem *Musée des Beaux Arts* he muses on Brueghel's Icarus and how everything, including the ploughman "who may have heard the splash" turned away "Quite leisurely from the disaster." Auden's Old Masters did not turn away from human suffering. Neither should we.

Endnotes

1 **Emil Zátopek** (1922-2000) "One of the greatest runners of the 20th Century,Emil Zátopek achieved legendary status when he won the 5,000, the 10,000 and the marathon at the 1952 Olympic Games in Helsinki.

"The Locomotive" or the "Bouncing Czech" as he came to be known, dominated long distance running from 1948 until 1954 when he won a remarkable 38 consecutive 10,000 meter races, including 11 in 1949 alone. He set 18 world records over various distances including every record from 5K to 30K, and won four Olympic gold medals and one silver. He was the first to run a 10K under 29 minutes and the first to run 20K in one hour." —*www.runningpast.com/emil_zatopek*

2 **Winter of 1944**"After the landing of the Allied Forces on D-Day [June 6, 1944], conditions grew worse in the Nazi occupied Netherlands. The Allies were able to liberate the southern part of the country, but their liberation efforts came to a halt when Operation Market Garden, the attempt to gain control of the bridge across the Rhine at Arnhem, failed. After the national railways complied with the exiled Dutch government's appeal for a railway strike to further the Allied liberation efforts, the German administration retaliated by putting an embargo on all food transports to the western Netherlands.

By the time the embargo was partially lifted in early November 1944, allowing restricted food transports over water, the unusually early and harsh winter had already set in. The canals froze over and became impassable for barges. Food stocks in the cities in the western

127

Netherlands rapidly ran out. The adult rations in cities like Amsterdam had dropped to below 1000 calories (4,200 kilojoules) a day by the end of November 1944. Over that winter, which has been etched in the Dutch people's memories as the *Hongerwinter* ("Hunger winter"), as the Netherlands became one of the main western battlefields, a number of factors combined to starve the Dutch people: the winter itself was unusually harsh and together with the widespread dislocation and destruction of the war, the retreating German army destroyed locks and bridges to flood the country and impede the Allied advance, this ruined much agricultural land and made the transport of existing food stocks difficult.

In search of food people would walk for hundreds of kilometers to trade valuables for food at farms. Tulip bulbs and sugarbeets were commonly consumed. Furniture and houses were dismantled to provide fuel for heating. From September 1944 until early 1945 approximately 30,000 Dutch people starved to death. The Dutch Famine ended with the liberation of the western Netherlands in May 1945. Relief efforts had shortly before been negotiated with the German occupiers and led to coordinated air droppings of food by the Royal Air Force over German-occupied Dutch territory in *Operation Manna*."
—*www.wikipedia.com*

[3] 1967 War and Yom Kippur War 1973

1967 War: The Six-Day War (Hebrew transliteration: *Milhemet Sheshet Hayamim*), also known as the **1967 Arab-Israeli War**, **Six Days' War**, or **June War**, was fought between Israel and its Arab neighbors: Egypt, Jordan, and Syria. It began when Israel launched what it considered a pre-emptive attack against Egypt, following the latter's closure of the Straits of Tiran to Israeli shipping and the deployment of troops in the Sinai near the Israeli border, and after months of increasingly tense border incidents and diplomatic crises. By its end Israel controlled the Gaza Strip, the Sinai Peninsula, the West Bank, and the Golan Heights. The results of the war affect the geopolitics of the region to this day."—*www.wikipedia.com*

Yom Kippur War 1973: "The Yom Kippur War, **Ramadan War** or **October War** (Hebrew:; transliterated: *Milkhemet Yom HaKipurim* or

Milkhemet Yom Kipur, Arabic:; transliterated: *Harb October* or transliterated: *Harb Tishrin*), also known as the **1973 Arab-Israeli War**, was fought from October 6 (the day of Yom Kippur) to October 24, 1973, between Israel and a coalition of Egypt and Syria. The war began with a surprise joint attack by Egypt and Syria into the Sinai and Golan Heights, respectively, which had been captured by Israel six years earlier during the Six-Day War.

"The Egyptians and Syrians advanced during the first 24–48 hours, after which momentum began to swing in Israel's favor. By the second week of the war, the Syrians had been pushed entirely out of the Golan Heights. In the Sinai to the south, the Israelis had struck at the "hinge" between two invading Egyptian armies, crossed the Suez Canal (where the old cease-fire line had been), and cut off an entire Egyptian army just as a United Nations cease-fire came into effect.

The war had far-reaching implications for many nations. The Arab world, which had been humiliated by the lopsided defeat of the Egyptian-Syrian-Jordanian alliance during the Six-Day War, felt psychologically vindicated by its string of victories early in the conflict. This vindication paved the way for the peace process that followed, as well as liberalizations such as Egypt's infitah policy. The Camp David Accords which came soon after led to normalized relations between Egypt and Israel—the first time any Arab country had recognized the Israeli state. Egypt, which had already been drifting away from the Soviet Union, then left the Soviet sphere of influence almost entirely." —*www.wikipedia.com*

[4] **Battle of the Bulge** The **Ardennes Offensive**, which was actually known to the Germans as ***Operation Wacht Am Rhein***, was also known as **Second Battle of the Ardennes** and popularly known as the Battle of the Bulge, started in late December 1944 and was the last major German offensive on the Western Front during World War II. The German army had intended to split the Allied line in half, capturing Antwerp, and then proceeding to sweep north to encircle and destroy four Allied armies, thus as Hitler believed, forcing the Western Allies to negotiate a peace treaty in the Axis' favour. The "bulge" refers to the extension of the German lines in this battle, forming a growing arc into allied controlled territory, seen clearly in maps presented in newspapers of the time.

Although ultimately unsuccessful, the offensive nevertheless tied down huge amounts of Allied resources, and the Allies' slow response to the resulting gap in their lines set their timetable back by months. However, the offensive also allowed the Allies to severely deplete the cream of the German army outside the defenses of the Siegfried Line and left Germany's remaining forces in a poor state of supply, thus greatly easing the assault on Germany afterward. In numerical terms, it is the largest land battle the United States Army has fought to date." —*www.wikipedia.com*

[5] **George Smith Patton, Jr.** (November 11, 1885 – December 21, 1945) A leading U.S. Army general in World War II. In his 36-year Army career, he was an early advocate of armored warfare and commanded major units of North Africa, Sicily, and the European Theater of Operations. Many have viewed Patton as a pure and ferocious warrior, known by the nickname "Old Blood and Guts", a name given to him after a reporter misquoted his statement that it takes blood and *brains* to win a war. But history has left the image of a brilliant military leader whose record was also marred by insubordination and some periods of instability. He once said, "Lead me, follow me, or get the hell out of my way."—*www.wikipedia.com*

[6] **Battle of Stalingrad** August 1942 - January 1943, "A major turning point in World War II, considered the bloodiest battle in recorded human history. The battle was marked by the brutality and disregard for civilian casualties on both sides. The battle is taken to include the German siege of the southern Russian city of Stalingrad (today Volgograd), the battle inside the city, and the Soviet counter-offensive which eventually trapped and destroyed the German Sixth Army and other Axis forces in and around the city. Total casualties are estimated at between 1 and 2 million. The Axis powers lost about a quarter of their total manpower on the Eastern Front, and never recovered from the defeat. For the Soviets, who lost almost one million soldiers and civilians during the battle, the victory at Stalingrad marked the start of the liberation of the Soviet Union, leading to eventual victory over Nazi Germany in 1945." —www.wikipedia.com

[7] **Montgomery** Bernard Law, 1st Viscount Montgomery of Alamein (1887–1976) British field marshal. "Educated at Sandhurst, he entered

the army in 1908 and served in World War I. In World War II he commanded (1939–40) the 3d Division in France until the evacuation of Dunkirk. In 1942 he was sent to Egypt to command the British 8th Army in Africa under the Middle Eastern Command headed by Gen. Sir Harold Alexander. Winning the battle of Alamein and driving the Germans 2,000 mi (3,200 km) across Africa into Tunisia made Montgomery an idol of the British public. He led the 8th Army in Sicily and Italy until Dec.1943. He helped formulate the invasion plan for France, and in the Normandy campaign he was field commander of all ground forces until Aug.1944, then led the 21st Army Group."
—*www.answers.com/topic/ bernard-law-montgomery*

"After the Allied landing in Normandy in June 1944, Montgomery directed all land operations until August, when the command was reorganized. He then took command of the Second Army Group, consisting of British and Canadian armies, which held the northern end of the Allied line. On September 1 he was made a field marshal, the highest rank in the British Army. Montgomery suffered his worst defeat of the war in September 1944 when his planned crossing of the Rhine at the Dutch city of Arnhem was turned back with the loss of 6,000 airborne troops. Responsibility for the debacle has been the source of continuing controversy.—*www.Grolier.com*

"When the Germans advanced in the Battle of the Bulge, he was given temporary command of two American armies. Afterward his troops thrust across N Germany to the Baltic, and he headed (1945–46) the British occupation forces in Germany. He was made viscount in 1946. He was chief of the imperial general staff from 1946 to 1948, when he became chairman of the commanders in chief in committee under the permanent defense organization of Britain, France, Belgium, the Netherlands, and Luxembourg. From 1951 to 1958 he was deputy supreme commander of the Allied forces in Europe. His writings include *Forward to Victory* (1946), *Normandy to the Baltic* (1947), *Forward from Victory* (1948), *El Alamein to the River Sangro* (1948), *An Approach to Sanity* (1959), *The Path to Leadership* (1961), and *A History of Warfare* (1968)."
— *www.answers.com/topic/bernard-law-montgomery*

8 Eichmann Trial "The Eichmann trial aroused international interest, bringing Nazi atrocities to the forefront of world news. Testimonies of Holocaust survivors, especially those of ghetto fighters such as Zivia Lubetkin, generated interest in Jewish resistance. The trial prompted a new openness in Israel; many Holocaust survivors felt able to share their experiences as the country confronted this traumatic chapter. Israeli attorney general Gideon Hausner signed a bill of indictment against Eichmann on 15 counts, including crimes against the Jewish people and crimes against humanity.

The charges against Eichmann were numerous. After the Wannsee Conference (January 1942), Eichmann coordinated deportations of Jews from Germany and elsewhere in western, southern, and northern Europe to [death] camps (through his representatives Alois Brunner, Theodor Dannecker, Rolf Guenther, and Dieter Wisliceny and others in the Gestapo). Eichmann made deportation plans down to the last detail. Working with other German agencies, he determined how the property of deported Jews would be seized and made certain that his office would benefit from the confiscated assets. He also arranged for the deportation of tens of thousands of Roma (Gypsies). Eichmann was also charged with membership in criminal organizations—the Storm Troopers (SA), Security Service (SD), and Gestapo (all of which had been declared criminal organizations at the 1946 Nuremberg Trial). As head of the Gestapo's section for Jewish affairs, Eichmann coordinated with Gestapo chief Heinrich Mueller on a plan to expel Jews from Greater Germany to Poland, which set the pattern for future deportations. For those and other charges, Eichmann was found guilty and sentenced to death. On June 1, 1962, Eichmann was executed by hanging. His body was cremated and the ashes were spread at sea, beyond Israel's territorial waters. The execution of Adolf Eichmann remains the only time that Israel has enacted a death sentence." —*www.ushmm.org*

9 Jewish New Year *Rosh Hashanah* is commonly known as the Jewish New Year. *Rosh Hashanah* occurs on the first and second days of *Tishri*. In Hebrew, *Rosh Hashanah* means, literally, "head of the year" or "first of the year."

September 23, 2006 (Jewish year 5767)
September 13, 2007 (Jewish year 5768)
September 30, 2008 (Jewish year 5769) –www.jewishvirtuallibrary.org

10 Queen Wilhelmina of the Netherlands (Wilhelmina Helena Pauline Marie of Orange-Nassau; August 31, 1880 – November 28, 1962), Princess of Orange-Nassau, Queen of the Netherlands from 1890 to 1948 and Queen Mother (with the title of Princess) from 1948 to 1962.

11 "Never again" See Samantha Power: Human-rights activist, lawyer, scholar, and writer. The author of *A Problem from Hell: America and the Age of Genocide,* a book on America's responses to the major genocides of the 20th century for which Power won the 2003 Pulitzer Prize for General Nonfiction. She currently is executive director of the Carr Center for Human Rights at Harvard University's Kennedy School. Power has said instead of "never again," we should be saying "again and again" because of the continuing genocides.

12 Kurt Weill and Bertoldt Brecht

Kurt Weill: (born Dessau, 2 March 1900; died New York, 3 April 1950). German composer, American citizen from 1943.

Son of a cantor, Weill was "a pupil of Humperdinck, Busoni and Jarnach in Berlin (1918-23); their teaching informed his early music, including the choral *Recordare* (1923) and the Concerto for violin and wind (1924), the latter also influenced by Stravinsky. But the deeper influence of Stravinsky, coupled with an increased consciousness of music as a social force, led Weill to a rediscovery in the mid-1920s of tonal and vernacular elements, notably from jazz, in his cantata *Der neue Orpheus* and one-act stage piece *Royal Palace*, written between two collaborations with the expressionist playwright Georg Kaiser: *Der Protagonist* and *Der Zar lässt sich photographieren.* In 1926 he married the singer Lotte Lenya, who was to be the finest interpreter of his music.

His next collaborator was Brecht, with whom he worked on *The Threepenny Opera* (1928), *The Rise and Fall of the City of Mahagonny* (1929) and *Happy End* (1929), all of which use … commercial music as a weapon of social criticism, though paradoxically they have become the epitome of the pre-war culture they sought to despise. Yet this is done within the context of a new harmonic consistency and focus. They explored other alternatives to the opera establishment in the school-opera *Der Jasager* and the radio cantatas *Das Berliner Requiem* and *Der Lindberghflug.* —*Grove Concise Dictionary of Music-online*

Increasingly uncomfortable with Brecht's restriction of the role of music in his political theater, Weill then turned to another collaborator, the famous stage designer Caspar Neher, for the libretto of his three-act epic opera, *Die Bürgschaft* (1931), and again to Georg Kaiser for the daring play-with-music *Der Silbersee* (1932). In both he refined his musical language into what he called "a thoroughly responsible style," appropriate for the serious and timely topics he addressed.

These later works outraged the Nazis. Riots broke out at several performances and carefully orchestrated propaganda campaigns discouraged productions of his works. In March 1933, Weill fled Germany; he and Lotte Lenya divorced soon thereafter. In Paris, Weill completed his Second Symphony and renewed briefly his collaboration with Brecht for *Die sieben Todsünden*, a "ballet with singing" for George Balanchine's troupe "Les Ballets 1933." He also wrote a number of cabaret chansons, as well as the score for Jacques Deval's *Marie galante*. When a German-language premiere of his *Der Kuhhandel* (libretto by Robert Vambery) seemed hopeless, Weill arranged for a London production of this operetta, which had been adapted as a British musical comedy and retitled *A Kingdom for a Cow*. In September 1935, Weill went to America, with Lenya, to oversee Max Reinhardt's production of Franz Werfel's biblical epic *Der Weg der Verheissung*, for which Weill had written an extensive oratorio-like score. After many delays, the work was finally staged in 1937 but in truncated form as *The Eternal Road*.

Then in 1935 he moved to the USA, where he cut loose from the European art-music tradition and devoted himself wholeheartedly to composing for the Broadway stage, intentionally subordinating aesthetic criteria to pragmatic and populist ones. Yet these works are still informed by his cultivated sense of character and theatrical form." www.kwf.org/pages/kw/kwbio

Bertoldt Brecht: (February 10, 1898 – August 14, 1956) An influential German dramatist, stage director, and poet of the 20th century. "Bertolt Brecht was born in Augsburg, Germany, on 19 February 1898. He studied philosophy and medicine at the University of Munich before becoming a medical orderly in a German military hospital during the First World War. This experience reinforced his hatred of war and influenced his support for the failed Socialist revolution in 1919.

After the war Brecht returned to university but eventually became more interested in literature than medicine. His first play to be produced was *Bael* (1922). This was followed by *Drums in the Night*, a play about a soldier returning from war, *Jungle of the Cities* (1923) and *A Man's a Man* (1926). In 1927 Brecht collaborated with the composer Kurt Weill to produce the musical play, *Mahagonny*. They then produced *The Threepenny Opera*. Although based on *The Beggar's Opera* that was originally produced in 1728, Brecht added his own lyrics that illustrated his growing belief in Marxism. He also worked with the composer Hanns Eisner in *The Measure Taken* (1930). Brecht attempted to develop a new approach to the theatre. He tried to persuade his audiences to see the stage as a stage, actors as actors and not the traditional make-believe of the theatre. Brecht required detachment, not passion, from the observing audience. The purpose of the play was to awaken the spectators' minds so that he could communicate his version of the truth.

Brecht's plays reflected a Marxist interpretation of society and when Adolf Hitler gained power in 1933 he was forced to flee from Germany. While living in exile he wrote anti-Nazi plays such as *The Roundheads and the Peakheads* and *Fear and Misery of the Third Reich*. This was followed by *Galileo* (1939), *Mother Courage* (1939), *The Good Man of Szechuan* (1941), *The Resistible Rise of Arturo Ui* (1941) and the *Caucausian Chalk Circle* (1943).

After leaving Germany in 1933, Brecht lived in Denmark, Sweden and the Soviet Union. He arrived in the United States in 1941 and after settling in Hollywood, helped with the writing of the film, *Hangman Also Die* (1943).

In 1947 the House of Un-American Activities Committee (HUAC), chaired by J. Parnell Thomas, began an investigation into the entertainment industry. The HUAC interviewed 41 people who were working in Hollywood. These people attended voluntarily and became known as "friendly witnesses". During their interviews they named nineteen people who they accused of holding left-wing views. Brecht was one of those named and after giving evidence to the House of Un-American Activities Committee, where he denied being a member of the American Communist Party, he left for East Germany

In 1949 Brecht founded the Berliner Ensemble and over the next few years it became the country's most famous theatre company. However, Brecht wrote only one new play, *The Days of the Commune* (1949), while living in East Germany. Bertolt Brecht died on 14th August, 1956." —*www.spartacus.schoolnet.co.uk*

[13] **Martin Adolf Bormann** Born 1930, the eldest son of Martin Bormann (June 17, 1900 – May 2, 1945) who was "a prominent German National Socialist (Nazi) official who became head of the Party Chancellery *(Parteikanzlei)* and Private Secretary to Adolf Hitler, gaining his trust and deriving immense power within the Third Reich by controlling access to the Nazi dictator. Martin Bormann and his wife, Gerda (who died of cancer in 1946), had ten children together, all of whom survived the war. Most were cared for anonymously in foster homes. His oldest son Martin Adolf was Hitler's godson. He became a Roman Catholic priest speaking out against Nazi abuses. Severely injured in 1969, he was nursed back to health by a nun. In 1971, they renounced their vows of celibacy and married. Mr. Bormann has been a tireless campaigner to preserve the memory of the Holocaust and oppose the activities of Holocaust deniers." —*www.wikipedia.com*

[14] **"Pippa Passes"** 1841, A song by Robert Browning (From *Pippa Passes*, a play)

> The year's at the spring
> And day's at the morn;
> Morning's at seven;
> The hillside's dew-pearled;
> The lark's on the wing;
> The snail's on the thorn:
> God's in His heaven—
> All's right with the world!

The above poem appears in the middle of Part I of the play *Pippa Passes*. —*www.potw.org/archive/potw48*

Ironically, Pippa's refrain, "God's in his heaven-/ All's right with the world!" is "often cited as the *reductio ad absurdum* of Victorian optimism. This sentiment, however, is clearly meant to characterize the girl's naïveté and childlike faith, and not the milieu in which she lives. For Pippa's world is given over to the tyranny of church and state, to corrupt officialdom, to envy and malice and wanton cruelty, to adultery and blackmail and murder. The society, which environs the girl from the silk mills of Asolo, makes a mockery of lawful love, patriotism, the familial relationships, and art. As she wanders the streets on her annual holiday, she brushes shoulders with pimps, prostitutes, debauched students, informers, hired assassins, and parasites of every variety. Her immunity to worldly degradation lies in her very unworldliness. She is a child of nature, unlettered, inexperienced, guileless, endowed only with a happy disposition, innocence, and the wisdom of her intuitions." —*www.victorianweb.org*

Film adaptation of *Pippa Passes* in 1909 by D.W. Griffith.—*www.nytimes.org*

[15] **Philip Glass** "An American composer, born January 31,1937. "His music is frequently described as *minimalist*, though he prefers the term *theatre music*. He is considered one of the most influential composers of the 20th century and is widely acknowledged as a composer who has brought art music to the public (apart from precursors such as Kurt Weill and Leonard Bernstein), in creating an accessibility not previously recognised by the broader market. Glass is extremely prolific as a composer and counts many visual artists, writers, musicians and directors among his friends, such as Richard Serra, Chuck Close, Doris Lessing, the late Allen Ginsberg, Robert Wilson, Godfrey Reggio, Ravi Shankar, David Bowie, and the conductor Dennis Russel Davies, who all collaborated with him. He is Buddhist and a strong supporter of the Tibetan cause. In 1987 he co-founded the Tibet House with Columbia University professor Robert Thurman and the actor Richard Gere." —*www.wikipedia.com*

By 1974, Glass had composed a large collection of new music for his performing group, The Philip Glass Ensemble, and music for the Mabou Mines Theater Company, co-founded by Glass. This period culminated in *Music in 12 Parts* (1974), a three-hour summation of Glass' new music, followed by the landmark opera, *Einstein on the Beach* (1976), a five-hour epic created with Robert Wilson that is now seen as a landmark in 20th century music-theater. This work, the first in Glass's "portrait" trilogy, was followed by *Satyagraha*, created for the Netherlands Opera in 1980, and *Akhnaten*, for the Stuttgart Opera in 1984. Over the years, Glass and Wilson worked on several other projects including *Civil Wars (Rome)* (1984), the fifth act of a multi-composer epic written for the 1984 Olympics; *White Raven* (1991), an opera commissioned by Portugal to celebrate its history of discovery and premiering at EXPO '98 in Lisbon and in 2001 at the Lincoln Center Festival, and *Monsters of Grace* (1998), a digital 3-D opera.

Beyond these landmark works, Glass' repertoire spans the genres of opera, orchestra, chamber ensemble, dance, theater, and film and includes collaborations with a variety of distinctive contemporary artists."—*www.schirmer.com/composers/glass_bio*

[16] **Ryszard Kapuściński** Born in 1932, in Pinsk, now in Belarus, "Kapuściński is the pre-eminent writer among Polish reporters. After honing his skills on domestic stories, he traveled throughout the world and reported on several dozen wars, coups and revolutions in America, Asia, and especially in Africa, where he witnessed the liberation from colonialism. He has devoted several books to Africa, including the *Heban (Ebony)*. After earning a reputation as an insightful reporter, Kapuściński amazed his readers in the 1970s with a series of books of increasing literary craftsmanship in which the narrative technique, psychological portraits of the characters, wealth of stylization and metaphor, and the unusual imagery served as means of interpreting the perceived world. Kapuściński's best-known book is just such a reportage-novel of the decline of Haile Selassie's anachronistic regime in Ethiopia—*Cesarz (The Emperor)*, which has been translated into many languages. *Szachinszach (Shah of Shahs)*, about the last Shah of Iran, and *Imperium*, about the last days of the Soviet Union, have enjoyed similar success....[His] tendency to process private adventures into a synthesis has made Kapuściński an eminent thinker, and the volumes of his *Lapidarium* are a fascinating record of the shaping of a reporter's observations into philosophical reflections on the world and people."
—*www.culture.pl/en/culture/artykuly/os_kapuscinski_ryszard*

[7] **Georges Eugène Sorel** (1847-1922) A French philosopher and theorist of revolutionary syndicalism, born in Cherbourg, son of a bankrupted wine merchant. He studied in the École Polytechnique in Perpignan, Sorel became chief engineer with the Department of Public Works and retired in 1892. He was active on the side of Dreyfusards during the Dreyfus Affair.

Sorel came to favour the anarcho-communism of Bakunin. Like Proudhon, he saw socialism as primarily a moral question. He was also heavily influenced by Henri Bergson who developed the importance of myth and criticized scientific materialism, by the cult of greatness and hatred of mediocrity found in Nietzsche, and by the ability to recognise the potential corruption of democracy found in liberal conservatives such as Tocqueville, Taine and Renan. Despite his disdain for social democracy, Sorel also held great respect for Eduard Bernstein, and agreed with many of his criticisms of orthodox Marxism.

He echoed the Jacobin tradition in French society that held that the only way for change to occur was through the application of force. Sorel praised Charles Maurras, *Action Française*, Lenin and Mussolini for attacking bourgeois democracy. At the time of his death, in Boulogne sur Seine, he had an ambivalent attitude about both Fascism and Bolshevism. Whether Sorel is better seen as a left-wing or right-wing thinker is disputed: the Italian Fascists praised him as a forefather but the dictatorial government they established ran contrary to his beliefs, while he was also an important touchstone for Italy's first Communists, who saw Sorel as a theorist of the proletariat. His ideas have contributed significantly to anarchosyndicalism.
—*www.wikipedia.com*

18 Milgram and Zimbardo

Stanley Milgram: "A psychologist at Yale University, [who] conducted a study focusing on the conflict between obedience to authority and personal conscience. He examined justifications for acts of genocide offered by those accused at the World War II, Nuremberg War Criminal trials. Their defense often was based on "obedience"—that they were just following orders of their superiors.

In the experiment, so-called "teachers" (who were actually the unknowing subjects of the experiment) were recruited by Milgram. They were asked [to] administer an electric shock of increasing intensity to a "learner" for each mistake he made during the experiment. The fictitious story given to these "teachers" was that the experiment was exploring effects of punishment (for incorrect responses) on learning behavior. The "teacher" was not aware that the "learner" in the study was actually an actor—merely indicating discomfort as the "teacher" increased the electric shocks.

When the "teacher" asked whether increased shocks should be given he/she was verbally encouraged to continue. Sixty percent of the "teachers" obeyed orders to punish the learner to the very end of the 450-volt scale! No subject stopped before reaching 300 volts! At times, the worried "teachers" questioned the experimenter, asking who was responsible for any harmful effects resulting from shocking the learner at such a high level. Upon receiving the answer that the experimenter assumed full responsibility, teachers seemed to accept the response and continued shocking, even though some were obviously extremely uncomfortable in doing so.

The study raised many questions about how the subjects could bring themselves to administer such heavy shocks. More important today are the ethical issues raised by such an experiment itself. What right does a researcher have to expose subjects to such stress? What activities should be and not be allowed in marketing research? Does the search for knowledge always justify such "costs" to subjects? Who should decide such issues?

Philip Zimbardo: The Stanford Prison Experiment—In the prison-conscious autumn of 1971, when George Jackson was killed at San Quentin and Attica erupted in even more deadly rebellion and retribution, the Stanford Prison Experiment made news in a big way. It offered the world a videotaped demonstration of how ordinary people middle-class college students can do things they would have never believed they were capable of doing. It seemed to say, as Hannah Arendt said of Adolf Eichmann, that normal people can take ghastly actions....

[The Experiment]—in summary: On Sunday morning, Aug., 17, 1971, nine young men were "arrested" in their homes by Palo Alto police. At least one of those arrested vividly remembers the shock of having his neighbors come out to watch the commotion as TV cameras recorded his hand-cuffing for the nightly news. The arrestees were among about 70 young men, mostly college students eager to earn $15 a day for two weeks, who volunteered as subjects for an experiment on prison life that had been advertised in the *Palo Alto Times*. After interviews and a battery of psychological tests, the two dozen judged to be the most normal, average and healthy were selected to participate, assigned randomly either to be guards or prisoners. Those who would be prisoners were booked at a real jail, then blindfolded and driven to campus where they were led into a makeshift prison in the basement of Jordan Hall.

Those assigned to be guards were given uniforms and instructed that they were not to use violence but that their job was to maintain control of the prison. From the perspective of the researchers, the experiment became exciting on day two when the prisoners staged a revolt. Once the guards had crushed the rebellion, "they steadily increased their coercive aggression tactics, humiliation and dehumanization of the prisoners," Zimbardo recalls. "The staff had to frequently remind the guards to refrain from such tactics," he said, and the worst instances of abuse occurred in the middle of the night when the guards thought the staff was not watching. The guards' treatment of the prisoners such things as forcing them to clean out toilet bowls with their bare hands and act out degrading scenarios, or urging them to become snitches "resulted in extreme stress reactions that forced us to release five prisoners, one a day, prematurely."

Zimbardo's primary reason for conducting the experiment was to focus on the power of roles, rules, symbols, group identity and situational validation of behavior that generally would repulse ordinary individuals. "I had been conducting research for some years on de-individuation, vandalism and dehumanization that illustrated the ease with which ordinary people could be led to engage in anti-social acts by putting them in situations where they felt anonymous, or they could perceive of others in ways that made them less than human, as enemies or objects." —*www.Stanford.edu*

19 "City upon a hill" A metaphor used to describe a utopia, for example, in Plato's *Republic* and Sir Thomas More's *Utopia*. Later, from John Winthrop's sermon "A Model of Christian Charity," 1630: "For we must consider that we shall be as a city upon a hill."

Ronald Reagan, "Farewell Address to the Nation," Jan. 11, 1989: "I've spoken of the shining city all my political life, but I don't know if I ever quite communicated what I saw when I said it. But in my mind it was a tall, proud city built on rocks stronger than oceans, wind-swept, God-blessed, and teeming with people of all kinds living in harmony and peace......" — *www.facsnet.org/issues/faith/civil_religion1*

[20] **Dostoevsky**, Fyodor, Russian author, one of his greatest novels is *The Brothers Karamazov* (1880), a masterpiece of literature with its moral struggle, showing the conflict between faith and doubt, reason and free will.

[21] Musa Dagh, Sobibor, Babi Yar, Belzec

Musa Dagh: "(*Musa Ler* in Armenian) was the site of the famed resistance during the Armenian Genocide [1915-1923]. Of the hundreds of villages, towns, and cities across the Ottoman Empire whose Armenian population was ordered removed to the Syrian desert, Musa Dagh was one of only four sites where Armenians organized a defense of their community against the deportation edicts issued by the Young Turk regime beginning in April 1915. By the time the Armenians of the six villages at the base of Musa Dagh were instructed to evict their homes, the inhabitants had grown suspicious of the government's ultimate intentions and chose instead to retreat up the mountain and to defy the evacuation order. Musa Dagh, or the Mountain of Moses, stood on the Mediterranean Sea south of the coastal town of Alexandretta (modern-day Iskenderun) and west of ancient Antioch.

With a few hundred rifles and the entire store of provisions from their villages, the Armenians on Musa Dagh put up a fierce resistance against a number of attempts by the regular Turkish army to flush them out. Outnumbered and outgunned, the Armenians had little expectations of surviving the siege of the mountain when food stocks were depleted after a month. Their only hope was a chance rescue by an Allied vessel that might be patrolling the Mediterranean coast. When two large banners hoisted by the Armenians were sighted by a passing French warship, swimmers went out to meet it. Eventually five Allied ships moved in to transport the entire population of men, women, and children, more than four thousand in all. The Armenians of Musa Dagh had endured for fifty three days from July 21 to September 12, 1915. They were disembarked at Port Said in Egypt and remained in Allied refugee camps until the end of World War I when they returned to their homes. As part of the district of Alexandretta, or Hatay, Musa Dagh remained under French Mandate until 1939. The Musa Dagh Armenians abandoned their villages for a second, and final, time when the area was annexed by Turkey.

In the face of the complete decimation of the Armenian communities of the Ottoman Empire, Musa Dagh became a symbol of the Armenian will to survive." —*www.armeniangenocide.org/Musa Dagh*

Sobibor: "[A death camp] Sobibor was established March 1942. First commandant: Franz Stangl. About 700 Jewish workers engaged temporarily to service the camp. Actually consisted of two camps divided into three parts: administration section, barracks and storage for plundered goods, [gassing], burial and cremation section. Initially, three gas chambers housed in a brick building using carbon monoxide, three gas chambers added later. Operations Began April 1942. Operations ended following inmate revolt October 14, 1943. Estimated number of deaths, 250,000, the majority being Jews....

In 1943, Jewish workers organized a resistance movement and worked out an escape plan. It was led by Leon Feldhendler. He was subsequently assisted by Alexander Pechersky, a Jewish officer in a transport of Red Army POWs which arrived in the camp in September 1943. The uprising was launched on October 14, 1943. In the fighting, 11 SS men and a number of Ukrainian guards were killed. Three hundred Jews escaped, but dozens were killed in the mine field around the camp and dozens more were hunted down over subsequent days. Of the Jews who broke out, 50 survived to the end of the war. The camp was liquidated in October 1943 and the site disguised as a farm."
—*www.jewishvirtuallibrary.org/sobibor*

Belzec: "Established November 1, 1941, Belzec extermination center [death camp] consisted of two camps divided into three parts: administration section, barracks and storage for plundered goods, and extermination section. Initially, there were three gas chambers using carbon monoxide housed in a wooden building. They were later replaced by six gas chambers in a brick and concrete building. Belzec [death camp] began operations March 17, 1942, and ended operations December 1942. The estimated number of deaths is 500-600,000, mainly Jews."
—*www.jewishvirtuallibrary.org/belzec*

Babi Yar: "By 1941, the focus and function of the *Einsatzgruppen* (mobile killing squads) had changed significantly. With the initiation of Operation Barbarossa, Germany's assault on the Soviet Union, the mobile killing units operated over a wide area of Eastern Europe from the Baltic to the Black Sea. There were four main divisions of the *Einsatzgruppen* — Groups A, B, C and D. These groups, all under Heydrich's general command, operated just behind the advancing German troops eliminating "undesirables: political "criminals," Polish governmental officials, gypsies and, mostly, Jews. Jews were rounded up in every village, transported to a wooded area, or a ravine (either natural or constructed by Jewish labor). They (men, women and children) were stripped, shot and buried. Sachar provides a description of one of the most brutal mass exterminations — at a ravine named "Babi Yar," near the Ukranian city of Kiev: Kiev ... contained a Jewish population of 175,000 on the eve of the Nazi invasion of the Soviet Union in 1941. The Nazi forces captured the city in mid-September; within less than a fortnight, on the 29th. and 30th., nearly 34,000 Jews of the ghetto were brought to a suburban ravine known as Babi Yar, near the Jewish Cemetary, where men, women, and children were systematically machine-gunned in a two-day orgy of execution. In subsequent months, most of the remaining population was murdered.

This, the most appalling massacre of the war, is often alluded to as a prime example of utter Jewish helplessness in the face of disaster. But even the few desperate attempts, almost comletely futile, to strike back served as a reminder that the difference between resistance and submission depended very largely upon who was in possession of the arms that back up the will to do or die." www.jewishvirtual library.org/babiyar

See also: "Babi Yar," a poem by Yevgeni Yevtushenko.

[22] **Lubavitcher** a member of a large missionary Hasidic movement known for their hospitality, technological expertise, optimism and emphasis on religious study.

[23] **Tall poppies:** successful people; **Tall poppy syndrome :** the tendency to criticize successful people.
—*www.koalanet.com.au/australian-slang*

[24] **Kipling's antisemitic poems** See "The Waster" or a later untitled

poem in which he warns people not to trifle "with Cohen from Jerusalem." (Ricketts 382).

25 Hutu Commandments Rwanda"The climax of state-sponsored racism came with the publication in December, 1990 of the notorious TEN HUTU COMMANDMENTS. These commandments appeared in *KANGURA* (Awaken) a newspaper owned jointly by the state and [President Juvénal] Habyarimana's [died 1994] top aides like Colonel Serubuga and late Colonel Sagatwa. Below we reproduce the full text.

1) Every hutu should know that a tutsi woman, wherever she is, works for the interest of her Tutsi ethnic group as a result we shall consider a traitor any hutu who marries a tutsi woman, makes a tutsi woman his concubine, ploys a tutsi woman as secretary or makes her his dependant.

2) Every hutu should know that our hutu daughters are more suitable and conscientious in their role of women, spouses and family mothers. Are they not beautiful, good secretaries and more honest?

3) Hutu women be vigilant and try to bring your husbands, brothers and sons back to reason.

4) Every hutu should know that every tutsi is dishonest in business. His only aim is to enhance the supremacy of his ethnic group. As a result, we shall consider a traitor any hutu forms an alliance with tutsi in business, invests his money or government's money in a tutsi's enterprise, lends or borrows money from a tutsi, gives favours to tutsi in business like obtaining of import licences, bank loans, construction plots, public markets, etc.

5) All the strategic posts, be they political, administrative, economic, military and security must be entrusted to hutu.

6) The education sector (pupils, students, teachers) must be majority hutu.

7) The Rwandese armed forces must be exclusively hutu. The experience of the october war has taught us a lesson. No military person should marry a tutsi woman.

8) The hutu should stop having mercy on the tutsi.

9) The hutu, wherever they are, must have unity, solidarity and be pre-occupied by the fate of their Hutu brothers the hutu both inside and outside Rwanda must constantly look for friends and allies for the Hutu cause, starting with our hutu brothers; They must constantly counter-act the tutsi propaganda. the hutu must be firm and vigilant against their common enemy who are tutsi.

10) The 1959 social revolution, the 1961 referendum and the hutu ide-ology must be taught to every hutu and at all levels. Every hutu must spread widely this ideology. We shall consider a traitor any hutu who will persecute his hutu brother for having read, spread and taught this ideology."
—*www.panafricanmovement.org*

[26] All the following are dictators who betrayed their people, killing oppo-nents and stealing millions and sometimes billions from their countries:

Pol Pot (1925-1998) Cambodia, Leader of the Khmer Rouge, Prime Minister (1976-1979), 1-3 million murdered during the Cambodian genocide.

Verwoerd, Hendrick Frensch (1901-1966) South Africa, Prime Minister (12958-1966) architect of apartheid, jailed Nelson Mandela.

Pinochet, Augusto (1915-) Chile, head of junta (1973-1990), many human rights violations, on trial.

Marcos, Ferdinand (1917-1989) Philippines, President (1965-1986), ruined economy and looted billions of the country's monies, rampant corruption, thousands killed.

Idi Amin (1925?-2003) Uganda, President (1971-1979), brutal regime,100,000-500,000 murdered, persecuted Asians and other tribes in Uganda, death squads.

Mugabe, Robert (1924-) Zimbabwe, President since 1980, corrupt, smashes opposition parties, steals land from both rich and poor, ruth-less.

Mobutu, Sese Seko (1930-1997) Zaire (now Democratic Republic of the Congo), President (1965-1997), executed political opponents, amassed a fortune at his country's expense.

APPENDIX

Timeline of the Destruction of Dutch Jews Germany occupied the Netherlands in May 1940. The Germans, at first formal and correct, quickly took a series of administrative measures that would tighten the noose around the Jews:

Jews were excluded from volunteer work in Germany as of July 1940. Jews were excluded from the civilian air guard at approximately the same time.

Jews were excluded from the civil service in August 1940 and if they were in the service, they could no longer be promoted. Dutch judicial authorities argued that these steps violated the Dutch constitution's anti-discrimination clause. Legal arguments were swept aside by further German orders.

All job holders in national, provincial, or local government had to sign an "Aryan declaration." In November 1940 Jews still in government jobs were suspended, in February 1941 they were fired. All Jewish businesses had to be registered by October 1941.

Jews were banned from movie theaters in January 1941 and prohibited from donating blood in February 1941.

In early 1941 Dutch national socialists in the NSB party began to harass Jews, especially in Amsterdam. After a Dutch Nazi died, the Jewish ghetto was closed off and, as punishment, the first Jews (387) were sent to Buchenwald on February 27, 1941. A few days later another 340 were sent to Mauthausen – none of these 340 would survive. Several other deportations would follow that year: 1941 was the year of the general rehearsals for what was to come.

The February 1941 events led to a strike in Holland, which was brutally suppressed: the period of an essentially "correct" occupation was over.

This year also saw the establishment of a Jewish Council of Jewish *prominenti*. Following the model established in Poland, the Council would keep order and social control, and act as the conveyor belt of anti-Jewish measures. In an atmosphere of fear and intimidation resulting from the original deportations, Jewish leadership felt that some form of "realistic collaboration" was the only option. It was not yet clear that the Germans saw the Council exclusively as a receptacle for German orders.[1]

A German bureaucracy for the Jewish questions, *Zentralstelle für jüdische Auswanderung*, was put in place by March 1941. The name was a euphemism for the systematic arrest of all Jews with an eye on the final solution. In June 1941 it was decided that the operation would be financed by the confiscation of Jewish property.

So, fifteen months before the planned deportations, everything was falling in place:

All Jews had been registered, given ID cards with a J, making them instantly traceable in July 1941; as of May 1941 they had to wear the yellow star.

Jewish assets had to be deposited with a savings bank controlled by Germans from which only small withdrawals could be made.

Jewish art possessions, jewelry, then bicycles were confiscated.

By early July 1941, Jews were told to shop only from 3 to 5 PM, to stop using public transportation, to stay out of non-Jewish institutions and homes, to give up their radios, to stay off the streets from 8 PM to 6 AM, and, in a routine letter from Adolf Eichmann, the first Dutch quota for deportation was established at 40,000, with the concession that 25,000 could be stateless Jews. The deportation was conveyed to the Jewish Council as a "labor transport" to Germany.

After a protracted period of negotiations, the Jewish Council managed to restrict deportation eligibility to those between 18 and 40, to prevent the separation of families, got the exemption of certain trade, and got an agreement that letters could be sent to those deported.

By July 1942 the deportation started in earnest—4,000 were called up but most did not show even when the Amsterdam police were brought in to find no-shows. *Razzias*, that means random arrest actions, followed. The Jewish Council pleaded with the no-shows to please go; otherwise, those arrested would be sent to concentration camps—and the news about hundreds of dead in Mauthausen had begun to trickle in. Some 1500 then showed up; after all, they were called to do labor, and it was sanctioned by the Jewish Council. Those randomly arrested were sent to Amersfoort, a Dutch camp, instead of Mauthausen. The Jewish Council had a Phyrric victory. The first transport to Hooghalen, near Westerbork, took place on July 14, 1942; 962 Jews were on the train: the second phase had begun.

The same month, July 1942, saw nine transports. By October 1942, the processing quarters became too small: the *Hollandse Schouwburg* (Dutch Theater) in Amsterdam became the new staging area. Once in Westerbork, certain categories of Jews were initially exempt but for those free for transport, as it was called, the stay could be as limited as 24 hours. Decisions about the size, destination and timing of transports were made by Eichmann's IV-B-4 Bureau in conjunction with its representatives in Holland, and with the camp commander in Westerbork—forty transports were completed in 1942.

From July 1942 to February 1943, 46,455 Jews were transported from Holland, all but a few thousand to Auschwitz. Of 42, 915 sent to Auschwitz in this period, 85 survived. Of those sent to other camps (3,540), 181 survived. The Jewish Council found out on September 8, 1942, that there had been "some deaths" in Auschwitz. By then, thousands had already died. Nevertheless, the Council decided to keep as many important people in Amsterdam as long as they could. Forced to operate as a state within a state, in complete isolation from Dutch society at large, the Council tried desperately to make thousands of exemptions, based on jobs, on origin, on social status, for example, half-Jews with kids. However, the only really significant interruption in the deportations, from December 1942 to January 1943, was due to the fact that railroad cars were needed for another job: to transport German soldiers on holiday leave.

In early 1943, Eichmann expanded the destination beyond Auschwitz, in particular, to Sobibor. The Nazis wanted to use new death camps such as Chelmno, Belzec, Treblinka, and Sobibor. In these camps there was, of course, no selection: most were murdered the day of arrival. Of 34, 313 Dutch Jews deported to Sobibor, 19 survived.

Exemptions became more restricted throughout 1943, and revisions took place in May, June, and September. By October 1, 1943, 88,000 Jews had been deported to Auschwitz, Sobibor, Mauthausen, Ravensbrück, and Buchenwald; another 11,000 were in Westerbork or other camps; 15,000 were still exempt, for example, those in mixed marriages and Jewish Council personnel; some 20,000 had gone into hiding; 3,700 had fled, 1,000 had legally immigrated.

In the very last phase of the war some privileged Jews ended up in Theresienstadt where, of 4,870 about 1,950, returned; 3,715 were sent to Bergen Belsen; 2,050 would survive. In the very last days of the war, Nazis would begin to see these Jews as possible bargaining chips. Of the total 107,000 Jews deported from the Netherlands, 5,200 survived.

"Befehlsempfänger für die Judenschaft," as Reichskommissar Seyess–Inquart called it; see Gerhard Hirschfeld, "Niederlande" in Wolfgang Benz, *Dimensions des Völkermords,* München: Oldensbourg, 1991, pp. 137 – 167. The summary of the anti-Jewish measures and deportation numbers provided in this appendix are largely based on the excellent summary of Hirschfeld.

Bibliography

Alexander, Yonah, and Michael S. Swetnam, *Usama bin Laden's al Qaida: Profile of a Terrorist Network*, Ardsley, NY: Transnational Publishers, 2001.

Appelfeld, Aharon, *The Story of a Life: Memoirs*, translation from Hebrew Aloma Halter, New York: Schocken, 2004.

Appleman Williams, William, *Empire as a Way of Life*, Oxford: Oxford University Press, 2000, rev. ed.

Armstrong, Karen, *The Battle for God: Fundamentalism in Judaism, Christianity and Islam*, London: HarperCollins, 2000.

Armstrong, Karen, *Holy War: The Crusades and Their Impact on Today's World*, New York: Doubleday, 1991.

Allison, Graham, *Nuclear Terrorism: The Ultimate Preventable Catastrophe*, New York: Times Books/Henry Holt, 2004.

Auden, W.H., *Poems*, selected by Edward Mendelson, New York: Borzoi, 1995.

Bacevich, Andrew J., *The New American Militarism*, Oxford: Oxford University Press, 2005.

Bar-On, Dan, ed., *Bridging the Gap: Storytelling as a way to work through political and collective hostilities*, Hamburg: edition Körber-Stiftung, 2000.

Bar-On, Dan, *Die > Anderen < in Uns – Dialog als Model der interkulturellen Konfliktbewältigung*, Hamburg: edition Körber-Stiftung, 2001.

Bauer, Yehuda, *A History of the Holocaust*, New York: Watts, 1982.

Bauer, Yehuda, *A History of the Holocaust: Revised Edition*, New York: Watts, 2001.

Hirschfeld, Gerhard, "Niederlande," in Wolfgang Benz, *Dimensions des Völkersmord*, München: Oldenbourg, 1991, pp. 137-167.

Blass, Thomas, ed., *Obedience to Authority: Current Perspectives on the Milgram Experiment*, Mahwah, NJ: Lawrence Erlbaum Associates, 2000.

Brickhill, Paul, *De Grote Ontsnapping*, transl. H.W.J. Schaap from The Great Escape (London: Faber & Faber, 1951), Utrecht: Prisma Boeken, 1961.

Browning, Christopher R., *Ordinary Men: Reserve Police Battalion 101 and the Final Solution in Poland*, New York: Harper Collins, 1992.

Buford, Bill, *Among the Thugs*, New York: Vintage Books, 1993.

Burns, Robert, *The Poetical Works of Robert Burns in one volume*, Leipzig: Bernhard Tauchnitz, 1845.

Buruma, Ian, "I didn't know about the Holocaust then – Growing up in Holland", in Devoldere, Luc, ed., *The Low Countries*, Rekkum: The Flemish Netherlands Foundation/Stichting Ons Erfdeel, (13) 2005, pp.100-109.

Campbell, Jeremy, *The Liar's Tale: The History of Falsehood*, New York: W.W. Norton, 2001.

Churchill, Ward, *A Little Matter of Genocide: Holocaust and Denial in the Americas 1492 to the Present*, San Francisco: City Light Books, 1998.

Colijn, G. Jan, "America vs. Europe: Emerging divergence in thinking about the Holocaust," *Proceedings*, Netherlands America Studies Association Conference, Amsterdam, 2004.

Colijn, G. Jan, "Carnage before our time: nineteenth century genocide," *Journal of Genocide Research* (2003) (4), December, pp.617-625

Colijn, G. Jan, "Hitler's Willing Neigbors – a review of Nanda van der Zee's *Om erger te voorkomen*, Amsterdam: Meulenhoff, 1997, *Holocaust and Genocide Studies*, vol. 11, nr. 2, Fall 1997, pp. 259-264.

Colijn, G. Jan, "The Politics of Memory and Anne Frank," Niebuhr Holocaust Education Guestship Lecture, Elmhurst College, March 1997, reprinted as Stockton College *Holocaust Resource Center working paper #5*.

Colijn, G. Jan, *et.al.*, ed., *The Netherlands and Nazi Genocide*, Lewiston, NY: The Edwin Mellen Press,1992.

Colijn, Helen, *De Kracht van een lied* (*Song of Survival; Paradise Road*), Franeker: Uitgeverij Van Wijnen, 1997, third ed.

Colijn, I., *Engels voor de H.B.S.-A*, Zutphen, W.J. Thieme & Cie, 1957.

Colijn, I., *England and the English*, Zutphen: W.J. Thieme & Cie, 1954, first ed., and 1962, third ed., edited by J. Boswinkel.

Colijn, I., *An Introduction to Shakespeare*, Zutphen: W.J. Thieme & Cie, 1958.

Colijn, I., *Rambles in Britain*, Zutphen: W.J. Thieme & Cie, 1953, first ed. and 1959, third ed.

Colijn, I., *Walks and Talks in the Fields of English Literature*, vol. 1 and 2, Zutphen: W.J. Thieme & Cie, 1958.

Colijn, I., *With the* M.M.S. *to England*, Zutphen: W.J. Thieme & Cie, 1956.

Conway, Martin, "Problems of Digestion: The Memory of the Second World War in Flanders," in Devoldere, *op.cit.*, pp.111-119.

Davis, Mike, *Late Victorian Holocausts*, London: Verso, 2001.

Durlacher, Gerhard, *Drowning: Growing up in the Third Reich*, London: Serpent's Tail 1994, reprint ed.

Durlacher, Gerhard, *The Search: The Birkenau Boys*, London: Serpent's Tail, 1998.

Durlacher, Gerhard, *Stripes in the Sky: A Wartime Memoir*, London: Serpent's Tail, 1992.

Eland, Ivan, *The Empire Has No Clothes: US Foreign Policy Exposed*, Oakland, CA: Independent Institute, 2004.

Ephimenco, Sylvain, *Hollandse Kost*, Amsterdam: Uitgeverij Contact, 1994.

Fredrickson, George M., *Racism: A Short History*, Princeton: Princeton University Press, 2002.

Freud, Sigmund, *Group Psychology and the Analysis of the Ego*, New York: W.W. Norton, 1975, revised ed.

Frey, Robert S., ed., *The Genocidal Tempation: Auschwitz, Hiroshima, Rwanda and Beyond*, Dallas: University Press of America, 2004.

Gans, M.H., *De Amsterdamse Jodenhoek in foto's 1900-1940*, Baarn: Uitgeverij Ten Haave b.v., 1974.

Garrett, Stephen A., *Ethics and Air Power in World War II: The British Bombing of German Cities*, New York: St. Martin's Press, 1996.

Gates Jr., Henry Louis, *Loose Cannons: Notes on the Culture Wars*, Oxford: Oxford University Press, 1993, reprint ed.

Goldhagen, Daniel J., *Hitler's Willing Executioners: Ordinary Germans and the Holocaust*, New York: Knopf, 1996.

Greene, Graham, *The Quiet American*, The Hague: William Heineman/Nederland, 1957, first continental edition, 2nd printing.

Gross, Jan T., *Neighbors: The Destruction of the Jewish Community in Jedwabne, Poland*, New York: Penguin Books, 2002.

Hayse, Michael, *et.al*, ed., *Hearing the Voices: Teaching the Holocaust to Future Generations, Proceedings of the 27th Annual Scholars' Conference on the Holocaust and the Churches*, Merion Station, PA: Merion Westfield Press International, 1999.

de Haan, Ido, *Na de ondergang: De Herinnering aan de Jodenvervolging in Nederland, 1945-1953*, The Hague: SDU, 1997.

Hedges, Chris, *War is a Force That Gives Us Meaning*, New York: Anchor Books, 2003.

Hershey, John, *Hiroshima*, New York: A.A. Knopf, 1985.

Hochschild, Adam, *King Leopold's Ghost*, Boston: Houghton Mifflin, 1998.

Hondius, Dienke, Return: *Holocaust Survivors and Dutch Anti-Semitism*, translation from Dutch David Colmer, Westport, MA: Praeger/Greenwood, 2003.

Howard, Michael, "Cold War, Chill Peace," *World Policy Journal*, vol. X, No.4, Winter 1993/94, pp.27-34.

Huyse, L., and Dhondt, S., *Onverwerkt verleden. Collaboratie en repressie in België, 1942-1952*, Leuven: Kritak, 1991.

Howe, Sir Geoffrey, *Conflict of Loyalty*, London: Palgrave Macmillan, 1995.

Jennings, Jeremy, ed., *Sorel: Reflections on Violence*, Cambridge UK: Cambridge University Press, 1999.

de Jong, L., *Het Koninkrijk der Nederlanden in de Tweede Wereldoorlog*, vol.1-13, The Hague: SDU Uitgeverij, 1969-1988.

Jünger, Ernst, translation from German Michael Hoffman, *Storm of Steel*, New York: Penguin Books, 2004.

Johnson, Chalmer, *Blowback: The Costs and Consequences of American Empire*, New York: Metropolitan Books, 2004.

Kapuściński, Ryszard, *The Soccer War*, translation from Polish William Brand, New York: Alfred A. Knopf, 1991.

Kapuściński, Ryszard, *Another Day of Life*, translation from Polish William R. Brand and Katarzyna Mroczkowska-Brand, London: Pan Books, 1987.

Katz, Steven T., *The Holocaust in Historical Context*, vol. I, New York: Oxford University Press, 1994.

Kershaw, Ian, *Hitler 1936-45: Nemesis*, New York: W.W. Norton, 2000.

Klima, Ivan, *Love and Garbage*, New York: Knopf, 1991.

Kohn, Murray J., *Is the Holocaust Vanishing?*, edited with an introduction by David Patterson, Lanham: Hamilton Books, 2005.

Kohn, Murray J., *The Voice of my blood cries out*, Vineland, NJ: Rival Publication, 2004.

Kundera, Milan, *The Book of Laughter and Forgetting*, New York: Harper Perennial Modern Classics, 1999, reprint ed.

Kuper, Simon, "Ajax, de Joden, Nederland," *Hard Grass – Voetbaltijdschrift voor Lezers*, number 22, March 2000, special issue.

Lakeman, Pieter: *Het Gaat Uitstekend – Zwendel en Wanbeleid in het Nederlandse Bedrijsfleven*, Weesp: De Haan, 1984.

Lakeman, Pieter, and Pauline van der Ven, *Failliet op Krediet – De rol van de banken in Neder land*, Weesp: De Haan, 1985, 2nd ed.

Lakeman, Pieter, *Frisse Zaken*, Amsterdam: Uitgeverij Balans, 1987.

Langeveld, Herman, *Schipper naast God, Hendrikus Colijn 1869-1944.*, vol. 2, 1933-1944,

Amsterdam: Uitgeverij Balans, 2004.

Leupen, Herbert, *Toeten en Blazen: Handboek voor Versierders*, Amsterdam: N.V. De Arbeiderspers, 1965.

Leydesdorff, Selma, *We Lived with Dignity: The Jewish Proletariat of Amsterdam, 1900-1940*, translation from Dutch Frank Heny, Detroit: Wayne State University Press, 1994.

Levinas, Emmanuel, *Otherwise than Being: or Beyond Essence*, Pittsburgh: Duquesne University Press, 1998.

Liempt, Ad van, *Kopgeld – Nederlandse premiejagers op zoek naar joden 1943*, Amsterdam: Balans, 2002.

Lipset, Seymour Martin, *American Exceptionalism: A Double-edged Sword*, New York: W.W. Norton, 1996.

Lijphart, Arend, *The Politics of Accommodation: Pluralism and Democracy in the Netherlands*, Berkeley: University of California Press,

1975, 2nd rev. ed.

Marrus, Michael R., and Robert O. Paxton. *Vichy France and the Jews*, New York: Basic Books, 1981.

Marrus, Michael R., *The Holocaust in History*, Hanover, NH: University of New England Press (for Brandeis University Press), 1987.

Miller, Arthur G., ed., *The Social Psychology of Good and Evil*, New York: The Guilford Press, 2005.

Miller, Judith, *One by One by One: The Landmark Exploration of the Holocaust and the Uses of Memory*, New York: Touchstone, 1991.

Milosz, Czeslaw, "Dostoevsky and Western Intellectuals," *Kultura*, January-February 1983, pp.151-156.

Minco, Marga, *The Glass Bridge*, London: Peter Owen Publishers, 1989.

Minco, Marga, *Bitter Herbs: A Little Chronicle/the Vivid Memories of a Fugitive Jewish Girl in Nazi-Occupied Holland*, New York: Penguin USA, 1991, reprint ed.

Moore, Bob, *Victims and Survivors: The Nazi Persecution of the Jews in the Netherlands*, London: Edward Arnold, 1977.

Mulisch, Harry, *Criminal Case 40/61, The Trial of Adolf Eichmann – An Eyewitness Account*, translation from Dutch Robert Naborn, Philadelphia: University of Pennsylvania Press, 2005.

Mulisch, Harry, *The Discovery of Heaven*, transl. Paul Vincent, New York: Viking, 1996.Mulisch, Harry, *Het Stenen Bruidsbed*, Amsterdam: De Bezige Bij, 1964, 14th ed.

Mulisch, Harry, *De Ontdekking van de Hemel*, Amsterdam: De Bezige Bij, 1992.

Mulisch, Harry, *De Zaak 40/61 – Een Reportage*, Amsterdam: Uitgeverij De Bezige Bij, 1962, 2nd ed.

Nival, Anne, *Chienne de Guerre: A Woman Reporter Behind the Lines of the War in Chechnya*, New York, PublicAffairs, 2001.

Novick, Peter, *The Holocaust in American Life*, Boston: Houghton Mifflin, 1999.

Nye, Robert A., *The Origins of Crowd Psychology: Gustave LeBon and the Crisis of Mass Democracy* in *the 3rd Republic*, Berverly Hills, CA: Sage Publications, 1975, 1992.

Pfaff, William, *The Wrath of Nations*, New York: Touchstone, 1994.

Pfaff, William, *The Bullet's Song: Romantic Violence and Utopia*, New York: Simon & Schuster, 2004.

Poliakov, Léon, *The Aryan Myth: A History of Racist and Nationalistic Ideas in Europe*, New York: Basic Books, 1974.

Power, Samantha, *A Problem from Hell: America and the Age of Genocide*, New York: Basic Books, 2002.

Presser, J., *Ondergang: De Vervolging en Verdelging van het Nederlandse Jodendom*, 1940-45, two volumes, The Hague: Staatsuitgeverij, 1965.

Presser, J., *Ashes in the Wind: The Destruction of Dutch Jewry*, Detroit: Wayne State University Press, 1968, 1988.

Reeve, Simon, *The New Jackals*, Boston: Northeastern University Press, 1999.

Ricketts, Harry, *Rudyard Kipling: A Life*, New York: Carroll & Graff, 2001 (paperback ed.).

Rittner, Carol, *et.al.*, ed., *Will Genocide Ever End?*, St. Paul: Paragon House, 2002.

Ruthven, Malise, *A Fury for God: The Islamist Attack on America*, London: Granta, 2002.

Spiegel, Fred, *Once the Acacias Bloomed*, Margate, NJ: Comteq, 2004.

Straus, Scott, "Contested meanings and conflicting imperatives: a conceptual analysis of genocide," *Journal of Genocide Research*, vol.3, number 3, November 2001, pp. 349-375.

Suaya, Laura, and Fred M. Fielding, *Mapping Internationalization on US Campuses*, Washington, D.C.: American Council on Education, 2003.

Simon, Paul, *The Tongue-Tied American: Confronting the Foreign Language Crisis*, New York: Continuum, 1988, reissue edition.

Talmon, Yaacov, *The Origins of Totalitarian Democracy*, Harmondsworth, Middlesex: Penguin Books, 1986.

van der Zee, Nanda, *Om erger te voorkomen*, Amsterdam: Meulenhoff, 1997.

van der Zee, Nanda, and Jacques Presser, *Het Gelijk van De Twijfel*, Amsterdam: Uitgeverij Balans, 1988.

Vonnegut, Kurt, *Slaughterhouse-Five, or, The Children's Crusade: A Duty Dance with Death*, New York: Vintage, 1991.

Wagner, Gottfried H., *Twilight of the Wagners: The Unveiling of a Family Legacy*, New York: Picador, 2000.

Wagner, Gottfried H., *Wer nicht mit dem Wolf heult*, Cologne: Kiepenheuer & Witsch, 1997.

West, Peter, "Mourning sickness marks a selfish culture," review of Matthew Taylor, *Conspicuous Compassion*, a report of the UK think tank Civitas, *Guardian Weekly*, February 26-March 3, 2004.

Williams, Paul. L., *The Al Qaeda Connection: International Terrorism, Organized Crime, and the Coming Apocalypse*, Amherst: Prometheus Books, 2005.

Wilson, James, *The Earth Shall Weep: A History of Native America*, New York: Atlantic Monthly Press, 2003.

Zimbardo, Philip G., *Stanford Prison Experiment*, Stanford: Philip G. Zimbardo, 1972.

DATE DUE

APR 21 2010	

GAYLORD   PRINTED IN U.S.A.